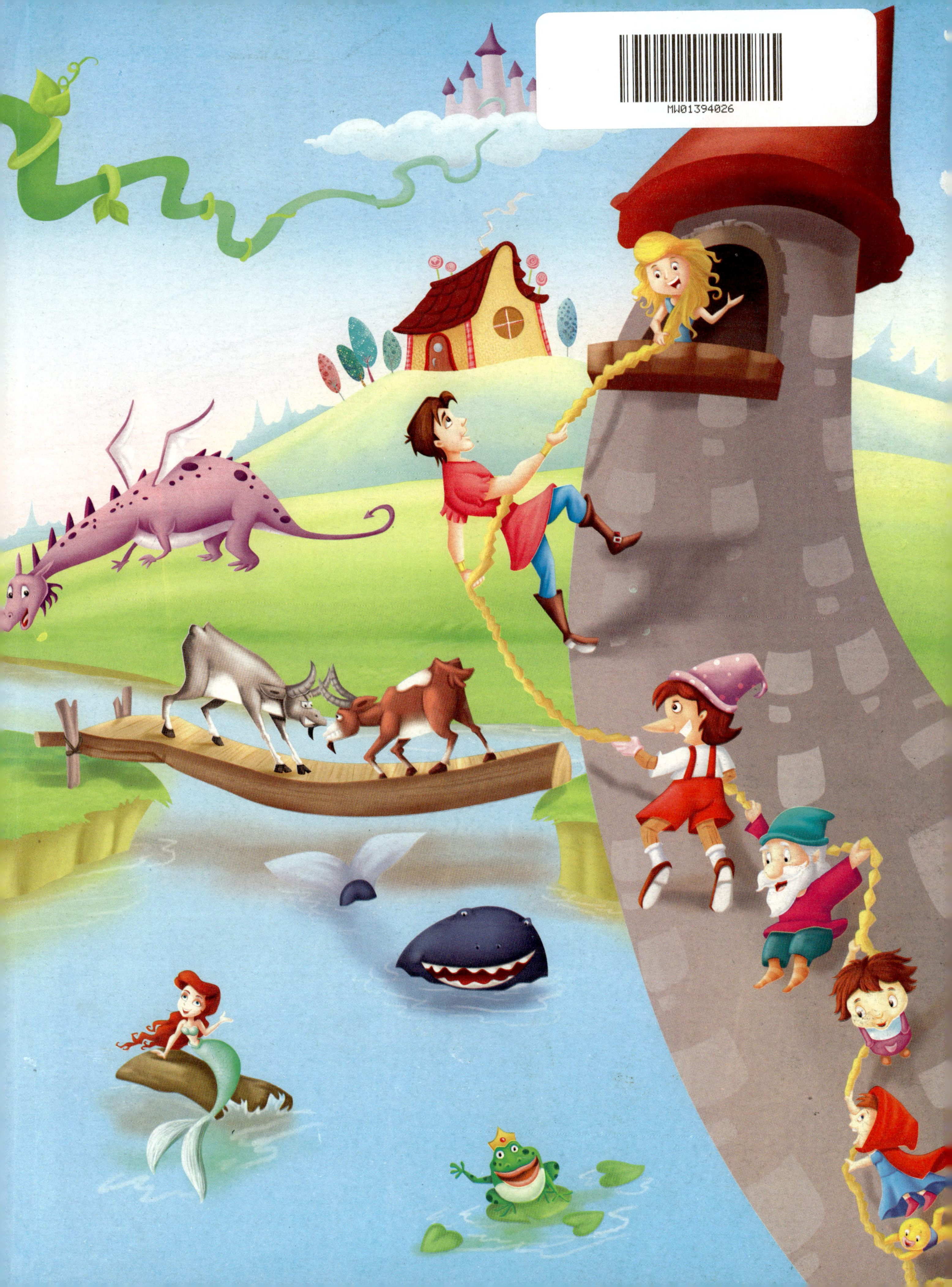

PEGASUS ENCYCLOPEDIA

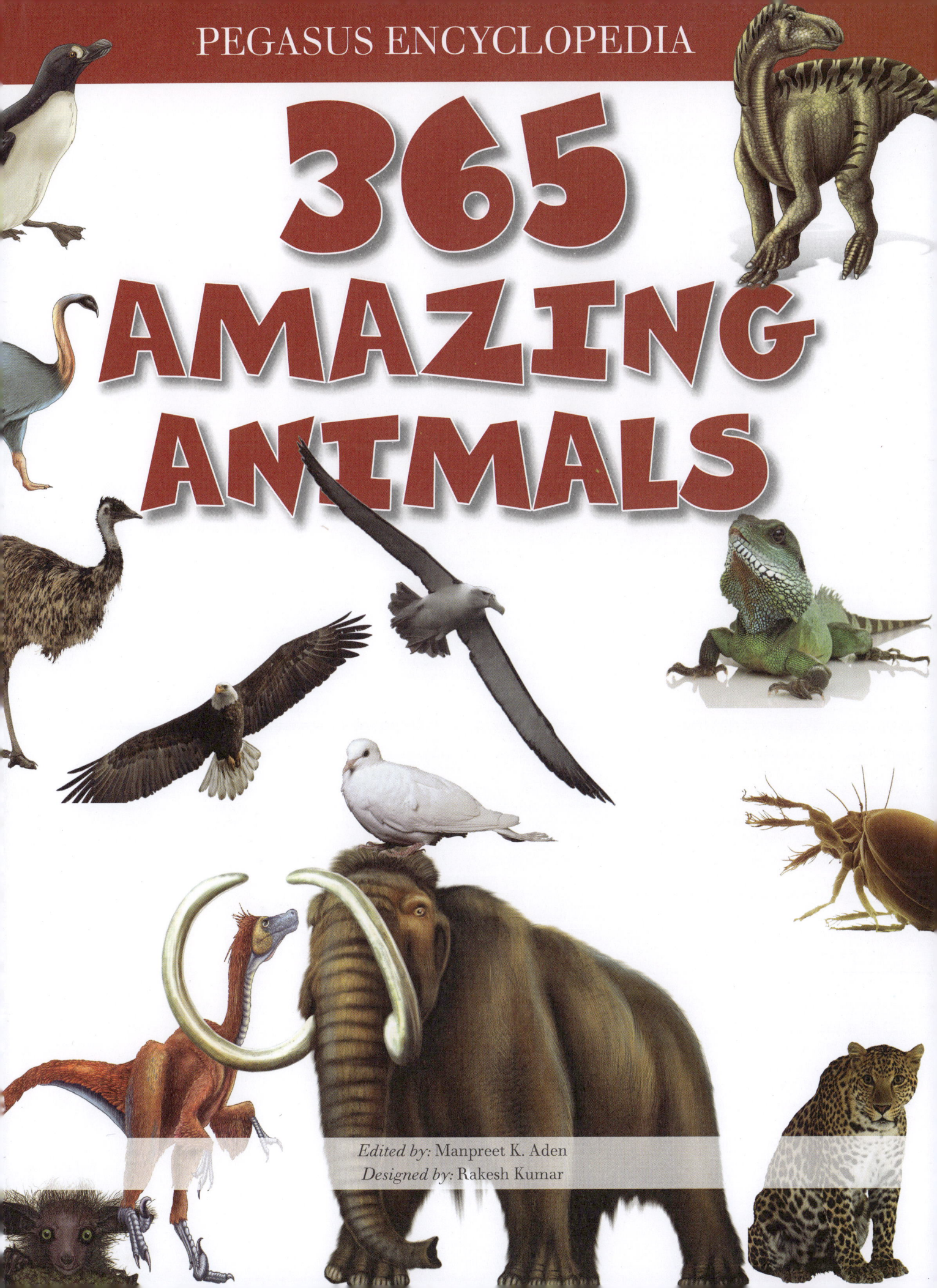

365 AMAZING ANIMALS

Edited by: Manpreet K. Aden
Designed by: Rakesh Kumar

All rights are reserved. No part of this book may be reproduced, stored in a retrieval system or transmitted, in any form or by any means, mechanical, photocopying, recording or otherwise, without any prior written permission of the publisher.

1st Impression

© B. Jain Publishers (P) Ltd.

Published by
Kuldeep Jain
for
Pegasus
An imprint of
B. Jain Publishers (P) Ltd.
An ISO 9001 : 2000 Certified Company
1921, Street No. 10, Chuna Mandi, Paharganj, New Delhi-110055 (INDIA)
Tel: 91-11-4567 1000 | Fax: 91-11-4567 1010
Website: **www.bjain.com** | E-mail: **info@bjain.com**

ISBN: 978-81-319-3251-3

Printed in India

CONTENTS

AMPHIBIANS

1.	African Clawed Frog	11
2.	Argentine Horned Frog	11
3.	Axolotl	12
4.	Blue Poison Dart Frog	12
5.	Budgett's Frog	13
6.	Cane Toad	13
7.	Chinese Giant Salamander	14
8.	Chinhai Spiny Newt	14
9.	Common Toad	15
10.	Darwin's Frog	15
11.	Emperor Newt	16
12.	Gardiner's Seychelles Frog	16
13.	Golden Toad	17
14.	Goliath Frog	17
15.	Malagasy Rainbow Frog	18
16.	Mallorcan Midwife Toad	18
17.	Mudpuppy	19
18.	Olm	19
19.	Oriental Fire-bellied Toad	20
20.	Pouched Frog	20
21.	Purple Frog	21
22.	Siberian Salamander	21
23.	Solomon Island Leaf Frog	22
24.	Southern Gastric-brooding Frog	22
25.	Spotted Salamander	23
26.	Spring Pepper Frog	23
27.	Taylor's Salamander	24
28.	Tomato Frog	24
29.	Waxy Monkey Leaf Frog	25

ARACHNIDS

30.	Black Widow Spider	26
31.	Deathstalker Scorpion	26
32.	Harvestmen	27
33.	Mites	27
34.	Orb Weaver Spider	28
35.	Scorpion	28
36.	Tarantulas	29
37.	Ticks	29

BIRDS

38.	African Grey Parrot	30
39.	Albatross	31
40.	American Crow	31
41.	American Flamingo	32
42.	American Robin	32
43.	Arctic Tern	33
44.	Bald Eagle	33
45.	Black Swan	34

46.	Blue Jay	34	70.	Mallard Duck	46
47.	Bluebird	35	71.	Marbled Murrelet	47
48.	California Condor	35	72.	Mockingbird	47
49.	Cardinal	36	73.	Nightingale	48
50.	Cassowary	36	74.	Nuthatch	48
51.	Cockatoo	37	75.	Oriole	49
52.	Common Rhea or Nandu	37	76.	Ostrich	49
53.	Crane	38	77.	Pelican	50
54.	Crested Oropendola	38	78.	Penguins	50
55.	Dove	39	79.	Peregrine Falcon	51
56.	Downy Woodpecker	39	80.	Philippine Eagle	51
57.	Duck	40	81.	Puffin	52
58.	Emperor Penguin	40	82.	Quail	52
59.	Emu	41	83.	Quetzal	53
60.	Golden Eagle	41	84.	Rainbow Lorikeet	53
61.	Great Egret	42	85.	Red-tailed Hawk	54
62.	Great Horned Owl	42	86.	Redbilled Oxpecker	54
63.	Gulls	43	87.	Roadrunner	55
64.	Harpy Eagle	43	88.	Rock Dove	55
65.	Hummingbird	44	89.	Rockhopper Penguin	56
66.	Junco	44	90.	Scarlet Macaw	56
67.	Kakapo	45	91.	Snow Goose	57
68.	Kiwi	45	92.	Snowy Owl	57
69.	Kookaburra	46	93.	Spix's Macaw	58

94. Spotted Owl	58	116. Ankylosaurus	70
95. Toucan	59	117. Argentinosaurus	71
96. Tree Sparrow	59	118. Brachiosaurus	71
97. Trumpeter Swan	60	119. Centrosaurus	72
98. Turkey	60	120. Chasmosaurus	72
99. Umbrellabird	61	121. Corythosaurus	73
100. Vulture	61	122. Deinonychus	74
101. Wandering Albatross	62	123. Dilophosaurus	75
102. Western Meadowlark	63	124. Diplodocus	75
103. Xenops	63	125. Giganotosaurus	76

CRUSTACEANS

		126. Iguanodon	76
104. Barnacles	64	127. Kentrosaurus	77
105. Coconut Crab	64	128. Lambeosaurus	77
106. Crab	65	129. Maiasaura	78
107. Crayfish	66	130. Mamenchisaurus	78
108. Hermit Crab	66	131. Nodosaurus	79
109. Krill	67	132. Ouranosaurus	79
110. Lobster	67	133. Pentaceratops	80
111. Mantis Shrimp	68	134. Sauropelta	80
112. Prawn	68	135. Spinosaurus	81
113. Shrimp	69	136. Stegosaurus	81
114. Woodlice or Pill Bug	69	137. Thecodontosaurus	82

DINOSAURS

| | | 138. Troodon | 82 |
| 115. Allosaurus | 70 | 139. Tyrannosaurus Rex | 83 |

140. Ultrasaurus	84
141. Utahraptor	84
142. Velociraptor	85

EXTINCT ANIMALS

143. Archelon	86
144. Arsinoitherium	86
145. Cryptoclidus	87
146. Desmatosuchus	87
147. Dodo	88
148. Dunkleosteus	88
149. Ekaltadeta	89
150. Elasmosaurus	89
151. Elephant Bird	90
152. Eohippus	90
153. Giant Moa	91
154. Keichousaurus	91
155. Macrauchenia	92
156. Megalodon	92
157. Morganucodon	93
158. Mosasaur	93
159. Nothosaur	94
160. Orthacanthus	94
161. Passenger Pigeon	95
162. Postosuchus	95
163. Quagga	96
164. Smilodon	96
165. Tasmanian Tiger	97
166. The Great Auk	97
167. Woolly Mammoth	98

FISH

168. Angelfish	99
169. Archerfishes	100
170. Basking Shark	100
171. Bluefin Tuna	101
172. Bony Fish	101
173. Clown Fish	102
174. Coelacanth	102
175. Deep Sea Angler Fish	103
176. Electric Eel	103
177. Goldfish	104
178. Great White Shark	104
179. Gulper Eel	105
180. Hatchetfish	105
181. John Dory	106
182. Lake Trout	106
183. Lantern Fish	107
184. Leafy Seadragon	107
185. Long-spined Porcupine Fish	108

186. Macropinna Microstoma	108
187. Manta Ray	109
188. Mushroom Scorpionfish	109
189. Piranha	110
190. Pufferfish	110
191. Pupfish	111
192. Red Lionfish	111
193. Salmon	112
194. Seahorse	112
195. Stonefish	113
196. Sun Fish	113
197. Swordfish	114
198. Whale Shark	114

INSECTS

199. Ant	115
200. Assassin Bug	115
201. Beetles	116
202. Blue Morpho Butterfly	116
203. Cicada	117
204. Crickets	117
205. Dragonfly	118
206. Firefly	118
207. Grasshopper	119
208. Harlequin Bug	119
209. Honey Bee	120
210. Housefly	120
211. Jumping Bean Moth	121
212. Ladybug	121
213. Leafcutter Ant	122
214. Mosquito	122
215. Pond Skater or Water Strider	123
216. Praying Mantis	123
217. Silkworm	124
218. Termite	124
219. Walking Stick	125
220. Wasp	125
221. Yellow Jacket Wasp	126

INVERTEBRATES

222. Corals	127
223. Jellyfish	128
224. Octopus	128
225. Sea Anemone	129
226. Sea Cucumbers	129
227. Sea Spiders	130
228. Sea Stars	130
229. Squid	131

MAMMALS

230. Aardvark	132

231.	African Elephant	132	255.	Chinchilla	145
232.	African Wild Cat	133	256.	Chipmunk	145
233.	Agouti	133	257.	Coati	146
234.	Alpaca	134	258.	Coyote	146
235.	Amazon River Dolphin	134	259.	Dall's Porpoise	147
236.	Antelope	135	260.	Deer	147
237.	Armadillo	136	261.	Duck-billed Platypus	148
238.	Aye-Aye	136	262.	Dugong	148
239.	Baboon	137	263.	Echidna	149
240.	Bactrian Camel	137	264.	Ferret	149
241.	Badger	138	265.	Flying Squirrel	150
242.	Bat	138	266.	Fossa	150
243.	Bear	139	267.	Fox	151
244.	Beaver	139	268.	Gazelle	151
245.	Bighorn Sheep	140	269.	Giant Otter	152
246.	Binturong	140	270.	Gibbon	152
247.	Bison	141	271.	Giraffe	153
248.	Blue Whale	141	272.	Gnu	153
249.	Bobcat	142	273.	Golden Lion Tamarin	154
250.	Bongo	142	274.	Gorilla	154
251.	Capybara	143	275.	Hares	155
252.	Caribou	143	276.	Hedgehog	155
253.	Cheetah	144	277.	Hippopotamus	156
254.	Chimpanzee	144	278.	Horses	156

279.	Hyena	157
280.	Jaguar	157
281.	Karakul	158
282.	Killer Whale (Orca)	158
283.	Leopard Seal	159
284.	Leopard	159
285.	Lion	160
286.	Llamas	160
287.	Lynx	161
288.	Mandrill	161
289.	Maui's Dolphin	162
290.	Meerkat	162
291.	Mink	163
292.	Mole	163
293.	Mongoose	164
294.	Moose	164
295.	Narwhal	165
296.	Okapi	165
297.	Orangutan	166
298.	Oryx	166
299.	Panda	167
300.	Pangolin	167
301.	Panther	168
302.	Polar Bear	168
303.	Porcupine	169
304.	Puma	169
305.	Raccoon	170
306.	Red Kangaroo	170
307.	Reindeer	171
308.	Rhinoceros	171
309.	Ring-tailed Lemur	172
310.	Ross Seal	172
311.	Siamang	173
312.	Slender Loris	173
313.	Sloth	174
314.	Snow Leopard	174
315.	Steller's Sea Cow	175
316.	Tapir	175
317.	Tarsier	176
318.	Tiger	176
319.	Walrus	177
320.	Weasel	177
321.	Wolf	178
322.	Yak	178
323.	Zebra	179
324.	Zorro	179

MARSUPIALS

325.	Bandicoot	180

326. Bilby	180
327. Kangaroo	181
328. Koala	181
329. Nabarlek	182
330. Numbat	182
331. Quokka	183
332. Quoll	183
333. Ringtail Possum	184
334. Sugar Glider	184
335. Tasmanian Devil	185
336. Virginia Opossum	185
337. Wallaby	186
338. Wombat	186

REPTILE

339. American Alligator	187
340. Black Caiman	187
341. Black Mamba	188
342. Cantor's Giant Soft-shelled Turtle	188
343. Chameleons	189
344. Chuckwalla	189
345. Desert Tortoise	190
346. Frilled Lizard	190
347. Gila Monster	191
348. Green Anaconda	191
349. Green Basilisk Lizard	192
350. Iguana	192
351. Indian Gavial	193
352. Inland Taipan	193
353. King Cobra	194
354. Komodo Dragon	194
355. Leatherback Turtle	195
356. Matamata Turtle	195
357. New Caledonian Giant Gecko	196
358. Nile Crocodile	196
359. Painted Turtle	197
360. Ploughshare Tortoise	197
361. Rattlesnake	198
362. Royal Python	198
363. Saltwater Crocodile	199
364. Sea Turtle	199
365. Slow Worm	200

1 African Clawed Frog

African Clawed Frog, also called Platanna, is found on the African continent. It is found at the bottom of rivers and lakes in eastern and southern Africa. It inhabits the stagnant as well as fast flowing rivers. It rarely leaves its habitat. It is called so because it has claws on its forelegs whereas its hind legs are webbed. It is also known to pop its head out of the water from time to time in order to breathe.

Interestingly, the African Clawed Frog is an excellent swimmer. It can literally swim in any direction. It uses its mottled skin as a camouflage to escape its enemies. The moment it sees its prey, without wasting time it grabs the prey in its claws. Did you know that it sheds its skin each season and even eats it!

AMPHIBIANS

2 Argentine Horned Frog

Argentine Horned Frog inhabits the rainforests of Argentina, Uruguay and Brazil. It is found in shallow waters. It is also known as the Pacman Frog probably because of its wide mouth. Its mouth is nearly half of its size!

It is mostly terrestrial. Is is about 6 inches in length. It has a large, round body with a big mouth and many teeth. A part of its upper eyelids cover its eyes to a certain point. It is an aggressive frog whose appetite for food never ends. It has a green coloured skin with black and red markings. When it feels threatened, it puffs itself and then screams loudly. It feeds on insects, small birds, mice and even lizards.

AMPHIBIANS

3 Axolotl

Axolotl is a salamander and it is quite unique. It inhabits the wetlands and canals near Lake Xochimilco near Mexico City in North America. The word Axolotl is thought to have its origins in the Aztec language.

It exhibits a unique trait called Neoteny. It means that this salamander does not develop adult characterstics but rather retains its tadpole like dorsal fin and its feathery gills, which are external, and stick out at the back of its wide head. It completely lives in water. It can be up to 30 cms in length. It feeds on insect larvae, worms, small fish and molluscs. It has a long life and it is extremely rare when an Axolotl develops into an adult.

4 Blue Poison Dart Frog

Blue Poison Dart Frog lives in the tropical rainforests of South America. It is among the most beautiful frogs, fascinating one so much that one wants to pick it up. This is something that one should not do. It is because this frog has a highly poisonous skin!

It has a sriking blue skin which is a warning to its predators that it is dangerous. Its skin is covered with glands that produce strong toxins. It is only about 5 cms in length. Its poison has been used by South American Indians to poison the tips of their arrows. It is mostly terrestrial but it is often found by a stream or a pond where the environment is dark and moist.

5 Budgett's Frog

Budgett's Frog, also known as the 'Hippo Frog', has a wide and comical face. It inhabits streams, rivers and ponds of Argentina and Paraguay.

It has a large, flattened body coloured with grey skin that is spotted with olive green or brown spots. Its a voracious eater and eats about anything. It can be 7-12 cms in length. Its small eyes are on top of its head whereby it can stay submerged in shallow waters with only its eyes sticking out as it waits for its prey. It is also called Freddy Kruger Frog because of its wide fingers with webs between them and aggressive nature. When it is frightened, it immediately opens its wide mouth and emits a shrill scream.

6 Cane Toad

Cane Toad are large and stocky amphibians. It inhabits the United States, South America and it was introduced in Australia in 1935. When it is under stress it can produce toxins in its parotoid glands and release them to kill its predators.

It has a dry and warty skin. It is heavily built and it can measure between 15-23 cms in length. Cane Toad is called so because it was introduced in Australia to check the population of the destructive cane beetle. It was thought that its toxins will destroy the beetles. But the experiment was a failure though the frog bred successfully.

AMPHIBIANS

AMPHIBIANS

7 Chinese Giant Salamander

Chinese Giant Salamander is the world's largest salamander. It inhabits the cold and fast moving streams and rivers in China. It spends all of its time in water.

It can grow up to 5.5 feet in length. It has a thick and smooth brown, green or black coloured skin with blotches on it. Though the larvae have gills, the adults breathe through the pores in their skin.

It has an elongated body with two pair of legs. It has poor eyesight. It however has sensory nodes on its skin which help it to detect its prey and also the difference in water temperatures. It is nocturnal and feeds on aquatic insects, small fish, shrimps and crabs.

8 Chinhai Spiny Newt

Chinhai Spiny Newt is quite secretive. It inhabits the forests on the low hills in China. It lives on land, hibernates and has a unique defence system.

It has a flattened body and head. It can measure up to 120-140 cms in length. It has knob like 12 glands on the sides of its body. It is usually brown or black in colour with orange markings on its tail. During winters it hibernates for five months. To defend itself its elongated ribs have its tips projecting out of its body. When caught and grabbed, it injects secretions into the mouth of its predator.

9 Common Toad

Common Toad, also known as the European Toad, is found in Europe, Northern Africa and Asia. It is found near ponds, rivers, streams and water reservoirs. It has a warty skin that distinguishes it from other toads.

It can be 8 cms in length. It has an olive green or brown skin. It can even change its skin colour according to its surroundings. It moves slowly while walking and often takes short jumps. As a defence mechanism, it secretes a toxic and foul smelling substance which discourages its predators to eat it. It is nocturnal and is mostly seen at dusk. Interestingly, it has been associated with witchcraft.

AMPHIBIANS

10 Darwin's Frog

Darwin's Frog was discovered by Charles Darwin while he was travelling through South America. This strange frog is found in Argentina and Chile. It is usually seen near cool forest streams and among the fallen leaves.

It has strange breeding habits. When the female has laid eggs, the male guards them and then weeks later, it places the eggs in its vocal pouch that extends along its body. The tadpoles develop in this pouch and hop out as tiny frog's weeks later.

It is also good at disguising itself. When threatened it rolls over and plays dead! It is about 2-3 cms in length. Its triangular head and its green and brown colour give it the appearance of a leaf!

15

AMPHIBIANS

11 Emperor Newt

Emperor Newt, also called Mandarin Newt or Mandarin Salamander, is found in the Yunnan region in China. It inhabits the forests and wetlands of the mountains of the region. It is also found in small ponds and sometimes in ditches.

It is a brightly coloured amphibian. It has a ridged head which is orange in colour. A bright orange coloured ridge also runs along its body. Orange coloured blotches also run along this ridge. It has a rough, dark coloured skin. The blotches contain poison glands. It can release the poison by expanding its rib cage. It can measure from 12-15 cms in length. It is an insectivore. It is most active at night.

12 Gardiner's Seychelles Frog

Gardiner's Seychelles Frog is probably the smallest frog in the world. It is even smaller than your thumbnail! It is native to the Mahe and Silhouette islands of Seychelles. It lives on the ground and likes to stay in moist and rocky areas.

It grows to only 11 mm in length. It is green to brown in colour with dark markings along its eyes, hind legs and the mouth. It has long hind limbs. It has a pointed snout and large eyes. Interestingly, its young do not hatch as tadpoles but rather as froglets. It is most active at night.

13 Golden Toad

Golden Toads were native to the rainforests of Costa Rica. Only the males of the species were golden. The last Golden Toad was seen in 1989. It is therefore thought to be extinct.

It was about 5-7 cms long. While the males were golden in colour, the females were dark in colour with red blotches. Usually, the males outnumbered the females. It was extremely sensitive to climate changes. The climate change is considered the reason for its extinction. It is also thought that it was infected by the same fungal infection that has decreased the amphibian population around the world.

AMPHIBIANS

14 Goliath Frog

Goliath is the largest frog in the world. It is found in the rainforests of western Africa around rivers and waterfalls. It can grow up to be 33 cms in length. It can be as big as a house cat!

It is most active at night. It is green in colour with a granular appearance. It has a variety of designs on its body. Interestingly, it does not have a voice sac like other toads and frogs. It has a long tongue that it can extend to catch its prey. It feeds on insects, fish and other amphibians. It is an able and fast swimmer and can leap to long distances. Its hands and feet are webbed. It prefers warm and humid temperatures.

AMPHIBIANS

15 Malagasy Rainbow Frog

Like its name, Malagasy Rainbow Frog is very attractive. It is native to the dry forests of Madagascar's Isalo Massif. It is seen in shallow pools found in canyons. It is well adapted to climbing rocks and even vertical surfaces.

Its skin is covered with a white, red, yellow and green pattern. Its skin is smooth except at the underbelly. It has a small mouth and large eyes. It can measure about 4 cms in length. It has vertical discs on its forefeet which allow it to cling to vertical walls. It has "claw-like" structures on its fingers which help it to improve its grip while it climbs. Its hind feet are webbed though it cannot swim properly. If threatened, it inflates itself to protect itself.

16 Mallorcan Midwife Toad

Mallorcan Midwife Toad is a tiny toad which is native to the Sierra de Tramuntana of northern Mallorca in the Balearic Islands, Spain. It is a strange toad where the male carries the eggs bound around its hind legs until the eggs hatch. It is also the reason for its name.

It has a large head and long legs compared to its tiny body. It is usually golden brown in colour with green or brown blotches on it. It has off-white underparts. A small triangle rests between its eyes. It can be about 4 cms in length. This strange species was first discovered in 1977. It is nocturnal and is often seen in crevices and under stones during the day.

17 Mudpuppy

Mudpuppy, also called waterdogs, is among the few salamanders that make noise. It is because of the noises, which are squeaky and resemble a dog's bark, that they are called waterdogs. It is found in southern Canada and midwestern United States. It inhabits the bottoms of lakes, ponds, rivers and streams.

It spends its day hiding under rocks, crevices and logs. It is about 41 cms in length. It is distinguished by its red external gills it develops as larvae and never sheds. It has a flat head and wide tail along with four toes on its stubby feet. It is brown or grey with blue or black spots. It never comes out of water.

18 Olm

Olm is a rare salamander that inhabits deep caves. It is found in the underwater caves and rives of southern Europe. As it spends all its life in underground lakes, it has a whitish appearance. It has a pinkish hue due to the blood capillaries near its skin and its internal organs can also be seen. It is also known as cave salamander, white salamander or human fish.

It is blind and finds its way and prey through a heightened sense of smell and sensors. It is about 30 cms in length. Though it has external gills, it also develops lungs. Interestingly, it can go without food for 10 years and lives a long life of 58 years.

AMPHIBIANS

AMPHIBIANS

19 Oriental Fire-bellied Toad

Oriental Fire-bellied Toad is native to Siberia, north-eastern China and Korea. Unlike other toads and frogs it cannot extend its tongue. It is found in slow moving rivers, streams and ponds. When out of water, it prefers the broad leaves of coniferous forests.

Unlike other toads or frogs, it leaps in air in order to catch its prey. It has a green coloured uppercoat with black blotches while its underbelly is bright red indicating that it is poisonous. It is about 5 cms in length. When threatened, its arches its back to display its bright underbelly as a warning. It hibernates from late September to May at the bottom of streams and under rotten leaves. Interestingly, its pupils are triangular.

20 Pouched Frog

Pouched Frogs inhabit the cool, moist and mountainous rainforests in Australia. It is usually seen under leaves and logs. It is only 2-3 cms in length. It has a grey, brown or red uppercoat. There are tiny pink spots at the base of each of its arms. A dark brown stripe goes from its nostril to the eye and runs down along its body.

Its feet are not webbed, instead its fingers and toes are swollen. Interestingly, it does not require water to breed and the female lays eggs on the ground. The males have pouches on their sides, where the tadpoles hatch until they have developed fully.

21 Purple Frog

Purple Frog is a rather recent discovery. It inhabits the Western Ghats of India. It is a familiar sight in the montane forests and the cardamom plantations. It is the only surviving member of an ancient group of amphibians that had evolved about 130 million years ago.

It has a large, bloated body that is grey and purple in colour. As compared to its body, it has a small face and small limbs. It is about 7 cms in length. It is well adapted to a burrowing lifestyle. It makes burrows in moist ground. It uses its hindlimbs as spades to thrown out the soil on its back. It is fond of termites and finds them using its long tongue.

22 Siberian Salamander

Siberian Salamander inhabits the harsh climate of the Arctic Circle near Kazakhstan and Mongolia. It is found in the coniferous and deciduous forests of the Taiga Zone near slow moving rivers and streams. It stays in biting cold by adapting its body to the environment around it.

Its body is either brown or olive grey coloured with dark spots on it. It has a long head and a flattened tail. It has four legs with four toes on each leg. It has a unique ability to combat cold. When temperatures become dangerously low, it allows its body tissues to freeze. It stays in this state for a long time, even decades.

AMPHIBIANS

AMPHIBIANS

23 Solomon Island Leaf Frog

Solomon island Leaf Frog are native to the rainforests of Solomon Islands and Papua New Guinea. It is a terrestrial frog. It can be either brown or green in colour. It is a unique frog because of its hatching ability.

Unlike other frog species, the young ones of this frog do not hatch as tadpoles but rather as tiny frogs. It has a long snout with horns. Its head has a triangular shape.

24 Southern Gastric-brooding Frog

Southern Gastric-brooding Frogs are another unique frogs. It is native to Queensland in eastern Australia. It inhabits rivers, pools and streams. This frog was first discovered in 1973.

It is unique in the way that the young of the species are hatched. The female swallows the eggs and keeps them in her stomach. During the time that the young ones are inside the females' stomach, she stops eating food and her digestive process shuts down. During this time, the females rely on breathing through their skin.

25 Spotted Salamander

Spotted Salamanders inhabit the lowlying forests in the United States and Canada. it is usually seen under logs and rocks. Though it has a large habitat but it is difficult to find a spotted salamander in its habitat. It has bright orange spots running along its black body. It measures about 23 cms in length. Like other salamanders, it too produces toxins in its glands to discourage its prey. It is most active at night. It feeds on insects, worms, spiders and millipedes.

26 Spring Pepper Frog

Spring Peeper Frog is found near ponds, streams and swamps in Canada and the United States. It is called so after the high-pitched peeping sounds that it produces after the spring thaw. It is a nocturnal frog and is rarely seen.

It has a vocal sac under its chin. To make its distinctive peeping sound, it fills the sac with air than releases the air forcefully. It makes the sound as it sits comfortably in soil or crevices, a practice which magnifies the sound. It has a brown skin with a dark 'X' marked on its back. It is between 2-4 cms in length. It has large toe pads for climbing trees. It hibernates during winters under logs and barks of trees.

AMPHIBIANS

AMPHIBIANS

27 Taylor's Salamander

Taylor's Salamander has some unique features. It inhabits only the Laguna Alchichica, a highly salty lake in Mexico. It is the only amphibian that can stay in water with such high salt levels. It is often found deep in the waters of Laguna Alchichica.

It has a flattened body with a wide head, a large mouth and smooth skin. Its tail is round and it never loses its external gills which it develops as a young. It has a yellow coloured skin with dark spots along its back and tail. It can eat about anything.

28 Tomato Frog

Tomato Frog is just like its name suggests. It is bright red in colour just like a tomato. It is found only on the large island of Madagascar. It is found near shallow pools, swamps and slow moving waters.

Despite being red, it has a black line starting from its eye and moving down its back. It is about 2-10 cms in length. It is also known for making burrows for hiding. When it is threatened it inflates itself resembling a tomato. It also releases a toxin from its skin when a predator puts it in its mouth. This toxin gums up the predator's mouth and eyes forcing it to release the frog.

29 Waxy Monkey Leaf Frog

Waxy Monkey Leaf Frog is native to Argentina, Brazil, Bolivia and Paraguay. It inhabits the savanna, shrub land and the forests. It spends all its time on trees. Instead of hopping like other frogs, it walks! It is therefore that it is called a monkey.

It has green skin with a waxy coating on it which prevents its skin from getting dry. It has long legs. It is about 8 cms in length. It has adapted itself to living on trees. While breeding, the female lays the eggs in the middle of a leaf and then folds the leaf. It suspends its nest from a branch over a stream so that the hatched tadpoles will drop into the water.

AMPHIBIANS

ARACHNIDS

30 Black Widow Spider

Black Widow Spiders are found in temperate climates around the world. It is distinguished by the hour glass shape on its abdomen. It is called so because the female kills and eats the male. It is extremely poisonous. Its poison is 15 times more poisonous than that of the rattlesnake.

The females are about 27 cms across with long legs. The males, however, are much smaller than the females. It has a hard exoskeleton and strong jaws. It makes its webs to attract its prey. It spins its web in dark places. When the prey has been caught in its web, the Black Widow Spider injects venom and digestive juices into its prey to kill it.

31 Deathstalker Scorpion

Deathstalker Scorpion is found in deserts and scrublands of Africa and the Middle East. Due to its appearance, it is either yellow or green; it seems like a plastic toy and harmless. However, it is extremely dangerous and the powerful venom in its stinger can be very painful. It is highly aggressive and would attack at the slightest provocation.

The female scorpion is 10 cms long while the male is slightly smaller. It is thin unlike the other scorpions. Its pincers are not powerful, so it is unable to grab its prey for long. As a result, it at once injects its pincers in its prey to kill it.

32 Harvestmen

Harvestmen are found in temperate and tropical climates. It is also called 'daddy longlegs' because of its extremely long legs in the context of its tiny body. Its legs have seven joints that help it to run rapidly over leaves and grass.

Its long legs, especially the second pair, are filled with sensors. Its legs act like our ears, nose and eyes. Its head, thorax and abdomen are all joined together. It can be 7 mm to 22 mm long. In order to defend itself from predators, it releases a stinking odour. Sometimes, it may detach one of its legs and still run to confuse the predator.

ARACHNIDS

33 Mites

Dust Mites inhabit our beds, carpets and furniture. Some also live on plants and animals and even in the soil. It is microscopic in nature and usually goes unnoticed. It feeds itself on the dead skin shed by humans and animals alike.

Dust Mites are harmless. It however carries allergens that can cause allergic reactions in some people. It is about 0.4 mm in length. It is blind though it has eyes. It has hair on its tiny body that help it to sense its surroundings.

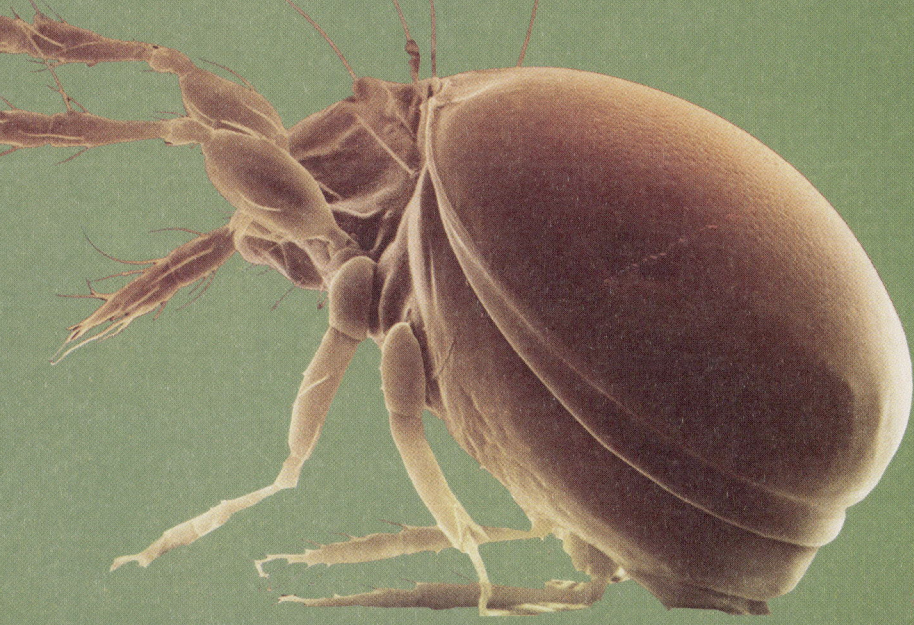

ARACHNIDS

34 Orb Weaver Spider

Orb Weaver Spider is found all over the world in warmer climates. This species varies in terms of size, colour and shape. It is called so because of the silk that it produces and uses to make its web. It weaves its web in circles and sometimes like the spokes of a wheel.

It is a brightly coloured spider with hairy legs. It has poor eyesight and uses the vibrations in its web to alert it of its prey. It mostly feeds on insects and small birds. It uses its venom to immobilize its prey. It also uses silk strands to weave its web.

35 Scorpion

Scorpions are found in a variety of climates. It inhabits deserts, forests, scrublands, caves and even lakes and ponds. Scorpions have inhabited the earth for the last 400 million years. It is among the few animals feared by humans.

Its appearance, where it has strong pincers at one end and a stinger with venom at the other, is enough to scare anyone. It is a nocturnal animal and is often seen in crevices and dark places. Though its venom is not harmful to humans, some species have venom powerful enough to harm humans. If food is scarce, a scorpion decreases its metabolic rate in order to survive. But still with lowered metabolism, it can spring quickly on its prey when it finds one.

ARACHNIDS

36 Tarantulas

Tarantulas are native to the warmer areas of North and South America, Asia, Africa and Australia. It is found in forests on the ground and in the trees and even in deserts.

Its large body that can be 12 cms long is covered with hair. It moves slowly and comes out mostly at night. Unlike other spiders, Tarantulas do not weave a web.

It feeds on insects but can even consume frogs and sometimes small birds. When a Tarantula has eaten a particularly large meal, it may not eat for a month.

It sheds its exoskeleton and in the process it can also replace some of its organs as well.

37 Ticks

Ticks are found in all parts of the world. It however prefers to stay in warm and humid climates. It is an external parasite. It feeds itself on the blood of mammals, birds and reptiles in order to survive.

It is a carrier of disease and causes great harm to the life-stalk. It can only crawl as it cannot fly or jump. It continues to feed on its host for several days. Once it has had its share of blood it drops off its host.

38 African Grey Parrot

African Grey Parrots are the largest parrots in Africa. It is native to the rainforests of West and Central Africa. It is usually found near clearings, forest edges and sometimes near mangrove forests. It is considered among the most intelligent birds.

African Grey Parrots have a pale grey plumage but their short tail is strikingly red. It has a black beak and yellow eyes. These parrots are well-known for their ability to mimic human voices. They can even learn words and can repeat them. It is, therefore, among the most beloved pets. Infact, a male African Grey Parrot called Prudle holds the world record for having a vocabulary of 1000 words!

BIRDS

39 Albatross

Albatross are large seabirds that are found in Antarctica, Australia, New Zealand, South Africa, South America, North Pacific and the Galapogas Islands. Albatross has the largest wingspan of any bird!

Albatross has a white body with a long neck and a short tail and legs. It is an excellent glider. With its large wings, it can reach upto 3.5 m in length. It can glide over the ocean for hours without flapping its wings. During rough weather, when high waves create strong uplifting air currents, Albatrosses can comfortably remain airloft for hours at end.

Albatrosses are often seen following ships for food and are well-known to sailors. They have also appeared in English Poet Samuel Coleridge's poem, *The Rime of the Ancient Mariner*. Did you know that Albatross drink the salty seawater!

BIRDS

40 American Crow

American Crows are found almost all over the continent. It has a jet black appearance. American Crows are seen in fields, on treetops, roadsides, fields and even on beaches. It is a social bird that gathers in large flocks. It makes a loud sound like a "caw".

American Crows live off the ground and eat almost anything. It is quiet aggressive and can even chase away large birds like hawks, owls and herons. It has a unique method of flying where it continuously flaps its wings and it very rarely breaks into gliding. Interestingly, when a group of crows are feeding, two sentinels are placed to keep a lookout for danger while the others eat!

41 American Flamingo

American Flamingoes are large pink birds that are always seen in large flocks. It is found in large, open, shallow ponds and lakes where the water is saline. It is quiet a noisy bird and when found in large flocks the variety of sounds they use to communicate are very loud.

American Flamingoes have a long neck and long legs. Its long bill turns downwards in the middle. It is pink in colour because of its diet. Carotene from the shrimps it feeds on gives its feathers their famous pink colour. Flocks of flamingos are often seen standing in water or wading but rarely swimming. Despite the bird's preference, American Flamigoes are strong swimmers. It can live upto 50 years!

42 American Robin

American Robin is a common songbird that is widely distributed all across North America. The early American settlers had mistaken it to be another species of the English Robin. It is however a species of thrush. It is often found in gardens and lawns where it is digging for earthworms.

This popular bird is often heard singing a merry song. It is easily recognizable by its orange breast and round body. When it is in lawns, it stands erect holding its beak upwards and is seen surveying its environment. During fall and winter, American Robin is seen flying in large flocks. These songbirds are also found in mountain forests and even in the Alaskan wilderness.

BIRDS

43 Arctic Tern

Arctic Terns are known for their annual migration. It makes the longest migration for any bird. It migrates from the Arctic Tundra to the Antarctic ice pack each year. It is thus that it always experiences longer days.

During its migration it covers a distance of 21, 750 miles! It is a social bird that lives in large groups. It has webbed feet, a long forked tail and a round head. It breeds in the Arctic Tundra. Before beginning its annual migration, the Arctic Terns which are usually noisy, become quite. Then these birds together take flight. This period before the flight is called "dread". While flying, an Arctic Tern merely swoops down to eat its prey which includes shrimps, insects and krill.

44 Bald Eagle

Bald Eagles, the national symbol of USA, are magnificent birds of prey. Bald Eagles are native to North America and are found near rivers and lakes. Though it is called a Bald Eagle but the bird isn't really bald. It is called so because of the white patch of feathers on its head. It had been the national symbol of USA since 1782.

The white patch on its head is in strike contrast to its dark brown feathers and wings. Its tail feathers are white while its eyes, beak and legs are yellow in colour. It is seen soaring in the sky and often flapping its wings near treetops. It is a carnivore. It makes large nests that are located on the treetops or on high cliffs.

45 Black Swan

Black Swan is native to the Australian continent. It has also been introduced in New Zealand and Sweden. It is found in shallow lakes, wetlands, wide rivers and also in flooded fields.

It has black feathers all over its body and a bright red beak. A layer of white feathers is also beneath the layer of black feathers. Unlike white swans, it does not migrate. It is extremely territorial and makes hissing and honking sounds when it feels threatened. Black Swans S-shaped neck is the longest neck among all the swan species! It flies in a V-formation. It feeds on water plants and grains. Interestingly, it molts each year which means it sheds its feathers after the breeding period. During this time it cannot fly.

46 Blue Jay

The Blue Jay is a noisy bird that can sing a variety of songs. It can interestingly also imitate other bird sounds. It has a beautiful blue plumage.

It has blue and white feathers with a white bar at the end of its wings. The shades of blue on its feathers look like mosaics when it is sitting. It is an intelligent bird and lives in complex social groups. These widespread birds are very fond of eating acrons. Blue Jays sometimes store the acrons in the ground to save them for later consumption. But often they forget about them. And this forgetfulness aids in spreading forests. Blue Jays are at their noisiest best when they are sitting on a branch but when flying they are usually silent. Its many calls usually carry over long distances.

47 Bluebird

Eastern Bluebird is a songbird. It sings in a melodic warble. It is native to eastern USA and southern Canada. It is easily recognizable by its striking blue colour. The bluebird has an orange or brown throat and breast and a white underbelly. It is greatly admired for its melodious and distinctive songs.

It is found in meadows. Bluebirds usually have two broods in a season. Sometimes, a young from the first brood stays in the nest to assist its parents in raising the second brood. This intelligent bird often sits on a branch when hunting, silently it watches its prey and then suddenly swoops down and captures it.

48 California Condor

California Condor is the largest bird in North America. It has a wingspan of about 3 metres. California Condor is a vulture. It can fly at altitudes upto 4,600 metres. Like other vultures, it too feeds on carrion. These large birds usually eat lots of meat in one go. This allows them to go without food for several days.

It is considered a sacred bird by the Native Americans. During the early 1980s' this large bird had come under the danger of extinction. With only a few dozen birds remaining in the wild, they were taken into captivity. With many measures, the population of California Condor has increased though the rate is slow.

BIRDS

BIRDS

49 Cardinal

The Cardinal is called so because of its red colour. It was named so by the native American settlers as the bird reminded them of Catholic Cardinals who wear bright red robes. Only males of the species have the distinct red colour. The females display a distinct grey colour. It is a song bird that is native to eastern USA and Mexico. It is also found in Hawaii.

The Cardinals are found in woodlands and often in backyards. It usually sings loud, whistling songs. It is aggressive by nature and territorial. It would not hesitate to attack other males who might intrude in its territory. It feeds on insects, maple sap and snails. It is a social bird and is often seen flying in flocks.

50 Cassowary

Cassowary is a large, flightless bird. It is native to Australia and New Guinea. It is the second largest bird in the world. It inhabits rainforests and swamps. The female Cassowary's are more brightly coloured than the males.

Cassowary usually prefers to stay alone except during the breeding season. This large bird is very territorial and can become very aggressive if threatened. It is also very secretive and therefore it is difficult to spot a Cassowary. It has a helmet like crest on its head and powerful legs. Its method to protect itself is by kicking. It can run upto 32 miles. A Cassowary can also jump upto 5 feet!

51 Cockatoo

Cockatoos are crested parrots that are native to Australia and Indonesia. They live in a variety of habitats including rainforests, dry areas and even fields. Cockatoos display a variety of colours including white the most common colour, yellow, pink and even grey and black.

It has a curved bill which distinguishes Cockatoos from other parrot species. It is a very smart bird and can easily learn tricks. Some Cookatoos even learn how to open their cages! It feeds on seeds, tubers, corns, fruit and flowers. Often Cookatoos are seen feeding in large flocks in the wild. It lives in tree hollows.

52 Common Rhea or Nandu

Common Rhea also called Nandu is a large flightless bird. It is native to the South American continent. It inhabits grasslands, savanna and grassy wetlands. It is a fast runner. When it runs, its neck is horizontal to the ground. It grows upto 5 feet tall and has long legs. It has large wings though they are useless for flight due to its large size and heavy body. However, it uses its wings to balance and change its direction when it runs.

It is a social animal and is often seen in groups of about 20-30 birds. It is opportunistic when it comes to eating. It does not leave a chance to eat when it gets near a farm or a field!

BIRDS

BIRDS

53 Crane

Cranes are among the largest birds in the world. They are found on all the continents except South America and Antarctica. They are usually found near wetlands with shallow water, wading through the water using their long legs.

When Cranes fly, they stretch their long necks to control their large bodies while flying. It is also because of their large bodies that the Cranes need a running start facing the winds. Cranes also migrate seasonally and they always fly in a V formation. It uses its sharp bill and long neck to kill its prey and to obtain tender plant roots. Interestingly, cranes have been symbols of wisdom, purity and prosperity and longitivity for thousands of years!

54 Crested Oropendola

Crested Oropendola is native to South America especially Panama and Argentina. It inhabits rainforests, grasslands, marshes and coastal regions. It is a small blackbird that is known for its loosely suspended nest.

It is covered in black feathers with yellow tail-feathers and a yellow beak. Its unique nest can be 3-6 feet in length. It makes its nest in the highest branches of the tree. Its nest is quiet large but it suspends its nest from a tree branch using only a few strands of fibres or grass. While the female hatches the eggs, the male protects their hanging nests from predators. Crested Oropendolas lives in large flocks that may contain as many as 100 birds.

55 Dove

Doves are a kind of pigeons. They are widely distributed around the world. They are commonly found in Australia and Asia. Doves hold a significant cultural importance around the world.

Doves are small but long tailed birds. It is a social bird and is often seen in groups. It mostly makes its nests on seaside cliffs or on the windowsills of tall buildings. These birds are also recognized by their cooing sound. Like pigeons, it also eats mostly seeds. Interestingly, it drinks water by sucking, an ability found in only a few birds. Doves are often released at important events and celebrations. Doves are harbringers of hope.

56 Downy Woodpecker

Downy Woodpecker is the most common and widespread woodpecker. It is widely distributed in North America. It is found in a variety of habitats including woodlands, parks and forests.

Downy Woodpecker is quiet small in size with black and white feathers and a short bill. The males of the species have a red spot on their head. This small woodpecker fastens itself to the tree trunks as it looks for food. It is often seen pecking at tree trunks to establish its territory. It also pecks to eat insects and when it has to make its nest. It makes its nest inside a hole in a tree.

BIRDS

BIRDS

57 Duck

Ducks are the most common water birds. Ducks are widely distributed around the world according to their species. Ducks are mostly seen wading in the water. It differs from swans and geese as it dives into the water to catch its food. It has a small, short neck and a wide bill. Its bill is quiet unique. Its bill allows the duck to forage through the muddy water and then strain the food from the water.

Its body is covered with feathers that have a waxy coating on them, making them waterproof. Interestingly, even if a duck remains underwater for some time, its feathers will remain dry! Do you know that contrary to popular belief not all ducks quack!

58 Emperor Penguin

Emperor Penguins are the largest penguins in the world. It inhabits only the Antarctic ice shield and thus inhabits the harshest climate on earth. Penguins are flightless birds but they are excellent swimmers. It can dive deeper than any other bird about 1,850 feet in the ice cold waters of Antarctica. It can stay underwater for twenty minutes.

The shape of their bodies helps them to survive. Beneath their outer feathers they have a layer of down feathers and a layer of blubber. The layer of down feathers keeps the cold air and water out. Also the oil in their bodies does not allow water to settle on their bodies. In order to stay warm, the penguins huddle together. When those at the bottom of the group have become warm, they step out and allow the others to get warm.

59 Emu

Emu is among the largest flightless birds in the world. It is found on the Australian subcontinent. It is usually seen in woodlands and shrub areas where there is plenty to eat and a good water source. Due to their heavy weight, Emu are unable to fly. Its body is covered with very soft feathers. It can grow upto 6 feet in length.

Emu do not stay at one place for long. It has a nomadic nature and keeps travelling in search of food. Due to its nomadic nature, it can adopt itself to the varying habitats. It is often found in flocks. It runs very fast and is also a good swimmer.

60 Golden Eagle

Golden Eagle is a powerful bird of prey. It is native to North America and is the national bird of Mexico. This bird of prey is recognizable by its brown-golden plumage. It has a powerful beak and its talons are razor sharp.

Golden Eagle is an extremely swift flyer. Once it has spotted its prey, it can dive upon it with a speed of upto 149 mph. It preys on small animals like rabbits, birds and fish. It can, however, even prey on large animals like deer. It usually builds its nest on high cliffs, tall trees and even on telephone poles. Its nests are usually large. It may come to the same nest to breed year after year.

BIRDS

BIRDS

61 Great Egret

Great Egret is a member of the egret family. This large wading bird is found in the Americas and also around the world. It is usually found near wetlands, streams, ponds and tidal flats. Its body is covered with white feathers. It is recognized by its long, S-shaped neck.

It spends its time patiently standing in the water, waiting for its prey to come. When the prey does comes by, with extreme accuracy, it captures and swallows it. It lives near water in large groups. It takes flight by slowly beating its wings and makes a deep croaking call.

62 Great Horned Owl

Great Horned Owl is called so because of the tufts of feather at its head. It is the largest owl in North America and is also native to South America. Its habitats include mountains, grasslands, forests and sometimes even deserts. It is the most distributed bird of prey in the Americas. Its far-carrying hoot is often heard in the evenings and at night.

It is a carnivore. It has a keen sense of sight and hearing which helps it to find its prey. It preys on rabbits, mice, squirrels, ducks and even skunks. It is an aggressive parent and even attacks those who come too near its nest. It usually takes hold of nests of other birds.

63 Gulls

Gulls, also known as seagulls, are distributed all over the world. They are found near the world oceans and inland waters. Gulls have white or grey feathers with varied markings on their heads or on their wings. Gulls have a strong bill which is slightly hooked at the end. Its wings are long and narrow and its feet are webbed.

Gulls are not only swift flyers but are also able swimmers. Gulls are often seen hovering near ship trails looking for refuse and around garbage bins. These birds are social and like to live in groups.

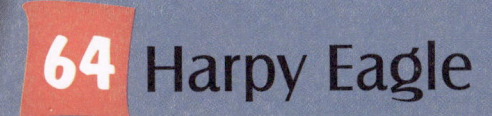

BIRDS

64 Harpy Eagle

Harpy Eagle is among the world's largest eagles and is a powerful bird of prey. It is native to the central and South American rainforests. It is named after the mythological harpies that had the face of a woman and the body of a bird. This large eagle has a wingspan of about 2 metres. It has a powerful hooked beak and massive talons. Its massive wings give it more agility when it flies. It wings also help it to move among the tree branches.

It has a loud whistling and clicking call. Its call can be described as *wheeeeeee* or *wheeeoooo*. It is usually seen in tropical and subtropical evergreen forests.

65 Hummingbird

Hummingbirds are tiny birds that beat their wings the maximum number of times. These tiny birds can even hover in mid-air. They are called so because when they fly, the flapping of their wings makes a humming sound. The Hummingbirds are native to North and South America. Did you know that Bee Hummingbird is the smallest bird in the world! It is the size of a bee!

Hummingbirds can beat their wings about 55-75 times per second! It feeds on plant nectar. It uses its long tongue to lap at the nectar. Interestingly, due to the structure of its wings, a hummingbird can not only fly forwards but also straight upwards, sideways and even backwards! The tiny legs of the Hummingbird do not allow it to walk or hop.

66 Junco

Junco is a small bird that is native to North America. It inhabits coniferous forests. During winters, it is also seen in parks and fields. These black eyed birds are very neat and look like little sparrows. It is easily recognizable by its flashy tail feathers that are clearly visible when the bird takes flight.

When on ground, it is usually seen hopping, looking for seeds and insects. During winters, these small birds are seen in flocks.

67 Kakapo

Kakapo is found only in New Zealand. It is probably the strangest parrot in the world. It is an endangered species and is a rare parrot. Kakapo is the heaviest parrot in the world and is flightless.

It has a green plumage that is downy and soft. It is a nocturnal animal and is rarely seen in daylight. Its plumage also allows it to hide itself on the forest floor. The male of the species produces a loud 'boom' sound during the breeding season that can be heard upto 5 kms away. However, its strong smell gives it away to its predators. Though the Kakapo cannot fly but it is a good climber and uses its small useless wings to balance itself.

68 Kiwi

The Kiwi bird is native to New Zealand. It is a flightless bird and is the national symbol of New Zealand. It inhabits forests, swamps, grasslands and farm lands. It is called so because of its unusual call.

Kiwi is the only bird in the world that has nostrils on its long bill. It is as big as a chicken. Its wings are so small that they are not visible beneath its feathers. It has a well developed sense of smell and hearing. It finds its food by using the sensory pads that are located at its bill. It comes out at night to eat but it is also seen sometimes during day.

BIRDS

69 Kookaburra

Kookaburra is native to the Australian continent. It is a large, noisy bird. It is the largest member of the Kingfisher family. It is also known as 'laughing kookaburra'. It is called so because of its loud, distinctive call which sounds like human laughter.

It has a dark brown plumage and white head and underbelly. Its red tail has patterned black bars. The kookaburras make a loud chorus at early dawn and dusk. It is therefore that they are also called 'bushman's clock.' It is a territorial bird that makes its nest in tree holes. Interestingly, the kookaburras do not drink any water. It gets all its water from the food it eats!

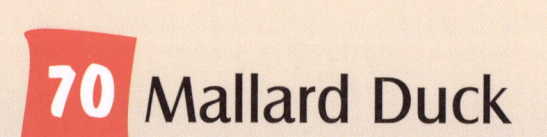

70 Mallard Duck

Mallard Ducks are the most common ducks in the wild. It is widely distributed around the world. It is often found in calm and shallow waters and even in brackish water and saltwater.

The males of the species are brightly coloured. They have a bright green head and brown neck with a white plumage and a yellow bill. The females, on the other hand, have a brown plumage and a brown bill. It is often seen dipping its head in the water. It spends most of its time on the surface of the water. It rarely dives in water. It feeds on small plants and grains.

71 Marbled Murrelet

Marbled Murrelet is a small seabird. It is mostly found near the coastline and bays of North America. It is an endangered species because of its habitat loss. The oil spills in the sea are also a threat to the survival of Marbled Murrelet. It is a small, chubby bird with a pointed bill and a pointed tail. It has a dark brown and white plumage.

It is a unique bird because of its nesting habits. It makes its nests on the largest trees of the coastal forests which are often far away from the coast. It makes a sharp 'keer' or 'kee' sound. It is a solitary bird.

72 Mockingbird

Mockingbird is a common songbird found all over the North American continent. It is found in a variety of habitats including farmlands, forest edges, open land, parks and even your backyard.

The Mockingbird is known for its ability to make a variety of calls. It has an amazing ability to mimic the calls of other birds. It can even sing a number of songs. Sometimes, it is even heard singing at night. Apart from its singing ability, it can also chase away other birds that intrude in its territory. It is fiercely protective of its young and eggs and can even attack when they are threatened.

It is a small bird with grey plumage with white patches at its tail and wings.

BIRDS

47

BIRDS

73 Nightingale

Nightingale is a small songbird. It is native to Europe and Central Asia. It inhabits the thickets of the deciduous forests. Nightingales are famous for their melodious songs. Its name means 'night songstress' in Anglo-saxon. It is called so because it is usually heard singing its loud, melodious songs at night.

It is a small bird which is often difficult to see. It is often found in the thickest branches of a tree. Its song only makes one aware of its presence. Its song is loud and complex with an impressive range of whistles and trills. It even makes its nest near the ground in a thick part of the forest.

74 Nuthatch

Nuthatch is a small, plump bird that is found in Europe. It inhabits the woodlands and coniferous forests. It has a blue-grey plumage at the top with orangish plumage on the sides. It is often seen hopping down a tree trunk extremely fast.

Nuthatch is a fast moving, acrobatic bird. It is called so after its habit of obtaining seed from a nut or acron. When it has found a nut, it places the nut in a crevice of the tree trunk. Then, it repeatedly hits the nut with its strong bill until the nut has opened and it has found the seed. Here, it uses its bill like a hatchet. It has a loud voice which often leads one to this hopping bird.

75 Oriole

Orioles are distributed all over the Americas. It is a small bird. Usually the males of the species are brightly coloured. Orioles are usually seen in woodlands and gardens. These small birds seem to prefer the warm regions.

Oriole is a shy bird and is not easily seen. However, their loud whistling and jarring notes are often heard. Oriole mostly feeds on insects though it also drinks flower nectar and fruits. It makes a hanging nest which is made of grass and tree bark. The nest is usually made between a fork in the tree branches.

76 Ostrich

Ostrich is the largest bird in the world. It is also the heaviest bird and it cannot fly. It is native to Africa and it inhabits the Savannah and the desert areas. Ostriches, however, can run very fast at about 43 mph.

Ostrich has long, powerful legs with two toes. With two toes, an Ostrich can achieve greater speeds. It has bare legs and neck while its body is covered with thick black feathers. When the ostrich runs, its wings act as rudders and helps it to change its direction. Despite the popular belief, Ostriches do not hide their neck in the ground when threatened. It instead falls down on the ground, extends its neck which blends with the ground. It thus appears from a distance that it has hid its neck in the ground.

BIRDS

BIRDS

77 Pelican

Pelican is a large bird that is found near coastal areas. It is found in the warm regions on all the continents except Antarctica. Pelicans also do not go or roam near deep waters.

Pelicans are famous for their unique beak. Its beak is about a foot long. Its beak's upper portion ends in a downward curved hook. Under its beak is a pouch like structure that is attached to its throat. Pelicans use this pouch to catch fish. While feeding, the pelicans roam over the water with their heads submerged in water to catch fish in their pouch. When the fish is caught, it tilts its bill downwards to drain the water and then swallows the fish. Interestingly, the Pelican's pouch capacity to hold water can be upto 3 gallons!

78 Penguins

Penguins are flightless birds that are native to Antarctica. The various species of Penguins inhabit the harshest climate on earth. Some Penguin species also inhabit the Galapogas Islands and are found near the equator.

Penguins have a stocky appearance and have very short legs. Their bodies are covered with a layer of blubber to protect them from the cold. Though the Penguins cannot fly, they are expert swimmers. They are known to make the deepest dives in the freezing Antarctic waters for any bird. They are also seen in large groups huddled together to keep each other warm. There large colonies are called 'rookeries'. All Penguin species are protected and they cannot be hunted and neither can their eggs be collected.

79 Peregrine Falcon

Peregrine Falcon is a bird of prey. It is widely distributed all over the world except in Antarctica. It can live in a variety of habitats. It is, however, found mostly near the coasts where the shore birds are in plenty. Its name means a 'wanderer'.

This bird of prey has blue or grey wings with brown plumage and brown spots on its white underbelly. It has a strong hooked beak and powerful claws. It is among the fastest flying birds in the world. When it has spotted its prey, it can dive at about 200 mph. In the past, its populations were greatly affected by the usage of DDT and other chemical pesticides. But when the usage of this pesticide was decreased or abolished, its populations increased rapidly.

80 Philippine Eagle

Philippine Eagle is among the largest eagles in the world. It is found on only 4 islands of the Philippines. This greatly endangered species is also known as the monkey-eating eagle.

It is greatly affected by the loss of its habitat which are the tropical forests. It can be easily distinguished by its elaborate headdress. It is often compared to a lion's mane. Its wingspan is about 2 metres long. Its chief food is monkeys, lemurs and snakes. It usually hunts in pairs. One Philippine Eagle acts as a decoy while the other swoops down in a sudden attack to catch their prey.

BIRDS

BIRDS

81 Puffin

Puffins are small sea birds that somewhat look like penguins. These birds live near cold Arctic coasts. These birds have a black and white plumage but their most distinguishing feature is their brightly coloured beak. Puffins are seen in large numbers near sea cliffs and on seacoasts.

Puffins can, unlike penguins, fly and even swim. Its beak is triangular and looks like that of a parrot. Interestingly, it digs burrows to lay its eggs. It can dive upto 200 feet in the sea. While flying, it flaps its wings 400 times per minute to reach a speed of 55 mph. Its chief food is fish.

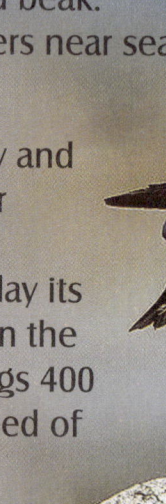

82 Quail

Quail is a medium sized bird that is found in various habitats. It is found in woodlands, desert edges, grass valleys and in chaparral. The bird, however, likes to stay in open areas and near brushy borders.

A Quail is a plump bird with a stocky body and pointed wings. Some species of Quails have a forward pointing head crest. Though it can fly but the Quail prefers to run instead. It even makes its nest on the ground. It produces a distinct sound that sounds like chi-CA-go where the middle sound is high pitched. It is usually seen in groups of a dozen or so. This group is called coveys. It mostly eats seeds, leaves and insects.

83 Quetzal

Quetzals are solitary birds that are native to Central America. Quetzal is a beautifully coloured bird. It is often considered one of the most beautiful birds in the world. They inhabit the mountainous and tropical rainforests of Central America.

Quetzal was a sacred bird to the Mayans and they have often depicted these birds in their art. Its colour also blends the bird with its surroundings making it difficult to be spotted. Despite their distinct colour, the male Quetzals also have long tail feathers. Its beak is also very strong. They are often seen perched on the tree canopies and it makes soft and deep calls depending on the situation.

84 Rainbow Lorikeet

Rainbow Lorikeet is a small Australian parrot. It is native to Australia and New Guinea. It inhabits forests, woodlands, mangrove forests and orchards. It is a brightly coloured parrot with a loud, shrill call and a bright red coloured curved bill. It is hard to tell apart the males and females.

It chatters while it eats. Rainbow Lorikeets are known for their comical antics. It feeds on insects, fruits, flower nectar, seeds and pollen. It is seen in a flock of about 20 birds. But they have been seen in flocks of hundred birds as well.

BIRDS

BIRDS

85 Red-tailed Hawk

Red-tailed Hawk is a bird of prey. It is the most widely distributed hawk in North America. Its habitats include deserts, swamps and woodlands among others. Red-tailed Hawks are usually seen soaring high up in the sky, slowly turning in circles.

It is a large, stocky bird. It has a brown plumage with a rust coloured tail. Its wingspan is about 4-5 feet long. When the wind is strong, it flies in the direction of the wind and it rarely flaps its wings. Red-tailed Hawks are very territorial and they often chase away other hawks that might come into their territory.

86 Redbilled Oxpecker

Redbilled Oxpecker is most commonly seen perched on the backs of other animals. It is native to sub-Saharan and central Africa. It inhabits the Saharan bushlands and forests of Africa.

It has a short, thick and red bill and bright yellow circles surround its eyes. It has a brown plumage while its undersides are yellow. This small bird is seen perched on rhinos, giraffes, elephants, buffalos and even zebras. While perched on the animals, it removes their ticks and fleas by eating them. Its style to find food is unusual in the animal kingdom.

87 Roadrunner

Roadrunner, also known as the Ground Cuckoo, is a fast-running bird. It is native to Mexico and Southwestern USA. It inhabits thorny scrub, sparse grasslands and desert areas. It can run upto 15 mph. This highly adaptable bird belongs to the cuckoo family.

Its plumage is brown with black and white feathers. It has a head crest and a long tail that is tipped with white feathers. It has four toes on its feet with two toes facing forwards and two facing backwards. When threatened, it flies but it cannot fly for a long time. Its call sounds like rattling and cooing.

88 Rock Dove

Rock Doves, also known as pigeons are native to Asia, North America and Europe. These birds are found in many cities apart from their habitat in the rocky cliffs, fields and farmlands.

Rock Doves usually have a dark grey plumage with light and dark grey stripes on their wings. It usually has purple or green shimmering colours on its neck. It is often seen in large flocks. When threatened or alarmed, the flock of pigeons rise together into the air and then they circle the area several times before they come down on the ground together. It makes a cooing sound.

BIRDS

BIRDS

89 Rockhopper Penguin

Rockhopper Penguins are small penguins that have a crest. These penguins are called so because they jump from rock to rock. It is among the world's smallest penguins and they inhabit the cliffs of the Antarctic islands.

They are easily recognized by their yellow and black crest, their blood red eyes and orange and red beak. They have a strong flipper like wings that allow them to make deeper dives. Rockhopper Penguins can dive upto 330 feet in pursuit of their prey. Their feathers are waterproof and their bodies are covered with three layers of short feathers that keep cold away from them. Interestingly, each year the penguins shed their old hair and grow new ones in a process called molting.

90 Scarlet Macaw

The Scarlet Macaw is a large parrot that is native to Central and South America. It inhabits the rainforests where it is usually seen in the canopy and the topmost branches of the trees. It is a colourful bird with vibrant colours in its plumage. Though, as its name suggests, the dominant colour in its plumage is red.

Its beak is large and powerful and its tail is very long and pointed. Its powerful beak can easily break nuts. Its long tail makes it appear quiet graceful. It is an intelligent bird and is very social. They can be found by their loud calls that sound like squawks and screams. It can fly with speeds upto 35 mph.

91 Snow Goose

Snow Goose is a migratory bird that inhabits North America. It breeds in the Arctic Tundra and then returns to the USA and British Columbia. They inhabit muddy fields and marshes. It is a strong flier and flocks of Snow Goose are often seen flying in a U-shape.

The plumage of Snow Goose is usually white but some can have grey to brown plumage. The brown to grey goose are called Blue Goose. It has a strong bill. When they fly in a large flock, they make honking calls and seem like white clouds. They are often considered to be harbringers of change. Snow Goose are usually seen in a flock whether on the ground or in air.

92 Snowy Owl

Snowy Owl also goes by the name of the Arctic Owl and the Great White Owl. It is a native of Canada, Greenland, Europe and Asia meaning that it prefers to live in the Tundra region. The Snowy Owl is also one of the largest owl species in the world.

It has a white plumage with some brown feathers in it. Usually, the males have completely white plumage but the females have brown feathers. They are usually perched near the ground waiting for their prey. It has sharp eyes and a keen sense of hearing. Interestingly, when their chief food, Lemmings population, is on the decline, the Snowy Owl does not lay eggs as food is scarce!

BIRDS

93 Spix's Macaw

Spix's Macaw are among the rarest birds in the world. It is believed that it has gone extinct in the wild as of 2000. Spix's Macaw was native to the north-eastern corner of the Brazilian rainforest.

Its plumage is blue-grey with a bright blue tail and ashy blue colour at its crown. The last individual seen in the wild was in 2000 and then it just disappeared. However, about 60 Spix Macaw survive today mostly in private collections. The reason for its decline is the loss of Caribbean Trumpet Tree on which it builds nests and also to perch. These trees are native only to Brazil. Also bird trade had led to its population decline.

94 Spotted Owl

Spotted Owls are native to the Pacific Northwest of USA and Canada. It inhabits the dense forests of the Pacific Northwest. It is a medium sized nocturnal owl. It has brown plumage with white spots and brown circles around its big brown eyes.

It is among the most studied owls. It makes its nests in the tree cavities to hide from the sun. When in the tree cavities, it also makes its famous call which goes like 'Whoop wu-hu hoo.' It is a predator and comes out at night to prey. It is a stealth hunter as it easily comes behind its prey without giving itself up. It is because its fluffy feathers provide it an almost silent flight.

95 Toucan

Toucan is a colourful bird with a brightly coloured long beak. It is native to South America and inhabits the tropical rainforests. It is a social bird that lives in small groups. It travels by hopping on trees and is a poor flyer.

The Toucans are known for their 7.5 inches long bill! Their bill is extremely colourful.

Its bill may deter its predator from attacking a Toucan but actually it is only for show. It mostly uses its bill to crack nuts. It has short but powerful legs. Toucans have a croaking call that sounds like RRRRK. Its bright colours also camouflage it among the dense tree foliage.

96 Tree Sparrow

Tree Sparrow is a widely distributed songbird in North America. It is smaller than a house sparrow and is known for its rapid and chirpy warble. It is frequently seen singing, picking seeds in the ground and perched on tree branches and scrubs and stocks. Tree Sparrows breed in northern Canada but they spend their winters in the United States.

It has a chest brown head, is plump and has a long tail. Small flocks of Tree Sparrows are seen often hopping on the ground and calling softly back and forth. Unlike other birds, it builds its nest near the ground and in depressions in the ground.

BIRDS

97 Trumpeter Swan

Trumpeter Swans are native to North America. It inhabits a variety of freshwater habitats including ponds, lakes and marshes. It is called so because of its loud and distinct call which goes 'oh-OH' and sounds like a trumpet.

Trumpeter Swans are migratory birds and they are also the largest swans in the world. It has a long white neck with white plumage and black beak and webbed feet. Did you know that they had become almost extinct about 100 years ago! But they were brought under the protection status and their populations are now increasing. It feeds on aquatic vegetation and sometimes aquatic fish.

98 Turkey

Turkeys can be domestic which are raised on farms and it can be wild which roams freely on forest floors, grasslands and swamps. Turkeys are native to North America.

Turkeys, only the males, have an elaborate display of ruffled feathers. It has a fan like tail, a bare head and a bright beard. The fanlike tail feathers are displayed during the breeding season. Turkeys have a distinct sound that can be heard a mile away. When alarmed, it runs rapidly. It can even fly but only for short distances. Interestingly, Benjamin Franklin wanted to make the Wild Turkey as the national bird of the United States instead of the Bald Eagle!

99 Umbrellabird

Umbrellabird is a unique bird that is native to Central and South America. It inhabits the continents rainforests. Umbrellabird is a migratory bird but instead of migrating from one land to another, it migrates to different altitudes in the mountain, going to higher altitudes.

Umbrellabird is called so because of the umbrella like crest on its head and a pendant shaped pouch on its throat. Its pouch can even be inflated and is inflated during the breeding season. The inflated pouch makes the bird look attractive and also makes its call louder! It has a black body with a broad bill. It is very difficult to see the umbrella bird as it lives on the highest branches of trees in the rainforests.

100 Vulture

Vultures are large birds of prey. They are widely distributed all over the globe except Antarctica and Australia. These long lived birds eat carrion and are solitary in nature.

Vultures are covered with feathers except on their head and neck. It has broad and powerful wings and it can fly for longer periods of time. It has strong sense of smell and sharp eyes. It can spot its food from miles away. Its beak is hooked and powerful. It uses its beak to tear the flesh, muscle and even bones of its prey! Vultures are among the highest flying birds! Though the bird is solitary by nature but groups of vultures are seen circling their prey in the sky.

BIRDS

BIRDS

101 Wandering Albatross

Wandering Albatrosses are seabirds that are known for their long flying. It continues to wander the ocean surface covering hundreds of miles and hence its name. It is native to the islands surrounding Antarctica. Wandering Albatrosses also have the largest wingspan of any birds at 11 feet!

Wandering Albatrosses are black and white in colour with stout bodies. Its long, narrow wings allow it to glide on the wind currents over the seas for days at end! It can even go without flapping its wings for hundreds of miles! Wandering Albatrosses are rarely seen on land except when they come to the land to breed. One Wandering Albatross was recorded to have travelled 3728 miles in 12 days!

102 Western Meadowlark

The Western Meadowlark is a brightly coloured songbird. It is native to North America and it inhabits fields, pastures, open grasslands and prairies. It sings a variety of songs which are quiet loud. It is rarely seen except when it is sitting on a fence post or a powerline and singing.

Western Meadowlark has bright yellow breast with a distinct V on it. It has a long and sharp bill and long legs. Its bright colours become dull in winters. It flies low. It makes its nests dome shaped with a side entrance.

BIRDS

103 Xenops

Xenops are small birds that are solitary in nature. These birds are widely distributed from southern Mexico to northern Argentina to central Brazil. Xenops inhabit the rainforests on the continent.

It usually roosts in tree holes and sings a fast and sharp sounding song. It has a small body with a long and flat, upturned bill. Using its upturned bill, it hammers on the decaying trunk of trees to roost and also to find food which are mainly insects without using its tail to support itself.

CRUSTACEANS

104 Barnacles

Barnacles, often confused with mollusc, inhabit the seas and oceans. It is often seen stuck to anchors, ship's bottom and rocks. Its body is made up of hard plates of calcium carbonate.

It is a filter feeder. It uses its curved feet, which stick out of its shell, to grab food and then pass it to its mouth. It cannot move on its own. It is seen flowing freely in the waters until it attaches itself to something hard. It can grow to be 1-7 cm in length.

Once it has attached itself to a hard surface, it produces a glue like substance that makes its hard shell thus giving it protection from the elements and the predators.

105 Coconut Crab

Coconut Crab is the largest land crab in the world. It is native to the islands of the South Pacific and is also found in the Indian Ocean. It is also called Robber Crab. It is not a true crab and is related to the Hermit Crabs. The young crabs of the species hide inside empty shells to protect themselves. The adults meanwhile develop a hard exoskeleton to protect its soft body.

It can be upto 1 m in length. It is a skilful tree climber. It eats fruits especially coconut and nuts. It has a keen sense of smell though it has poor eyesight. It likes shiny objects and often takes away shiny things. It is therefore also called a robber crab.

CRUSTACEANS

106 Crab

Crabs are found near the coastal areas around the world. Depending on the species, crabs live either in water or on land. It can live both in seawater and in freshwater.

It has a thick shell that protects its soft body. In the absence of a backbone, the shell also supports its body. It has two powerful pincers and eight legs. It uses its pincers to grab its prey. It has two eyes which are located on small stalks. Interestingly, crabs walk sideways. It can vary from a few mm to a few metres in length. Marine crabs breathe through gills while those on lands have two cavities in their bodies that act like lungs.

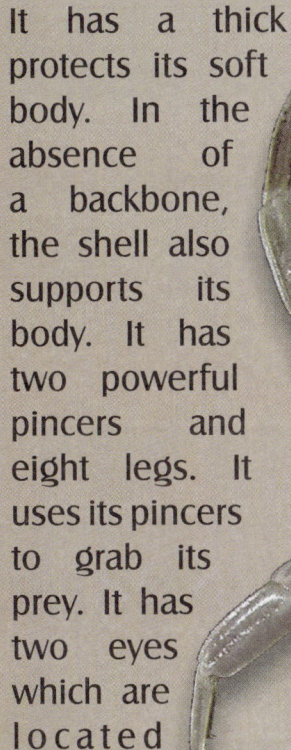

CRUSTACEANS

107 Crayfish

Crayfish is found around the world in freshwaters including ponds, rivers and streams. Though it resembles lobster, it is not a lobster. Most Crayfish are aquatic but some are semi-aquatic. In order to breathe, some semi aquatic Crayfish dig into the soil to reach water.

It too has eight legs with two powerful claws and its body is protected by a shell. Its colour varies from orange, brown to red. It can regrow its broken leg. It is most active at night. When threatened, it raises its powerful claws to threaten its predator.

108 Hermit Crab

Hermit Crab is called so because it lives inside a shell. The shell gives protection to its body. It is not a true crab as it does not have a hard shell to protect itself, especially its abdomen. It lives on the ocean floor. A few Hermit Crab species also live on land. As it grows, it must continue to find bigger shells to accommodate its growing body.

It can range in colour from red, brown, purple to orange and yellow. Like true crabs it has eight legs and two powerful claws. It is an omnivore. It can be 2-10 cms in length.

109 Krill

Krill are tiny animals that inhabit all the oceans of the world. It is the most important food source for a number of marine animals. It is a translucent, slightly pink animal which stays at great depths in the sea to escape its predators. It comes to the sea surface at night to eat phytoplankton.

It is sometimes seen floating in the sea in dense pink swarms. It is 1-14 cms in length. The Antarctic Krill is thought to be the most important among all the krill. It has a hard exoskeleton and many legs which help it in swimming. Interestingly, krill can live for 10 years.

CRUSTACEANS

110 Lobster

Lobsters are found on the ocean floor. It is found in all the oceans. Some lobster species are also found in freshwater. It too like crabs lacks a backbone. It is a cold blooded animal. Did you know that its body temperature depends on the temperature of the water!

It has four pairs of legs, two large powerful claws and a tail fan. It is a carnivore and comes out only at night to eat. It has poor eyesight but enhanced senses of smell and taste. It continues to grow all its life and it must shed its shells to grow. It lives among rock crevices, burrows and often near sea grasses.

CRUSTACEANS

111 Mantis Shrimp

Mantis Shrimp are small crustaceans that are found in tropical and subtropical seas around the world. It is mostly seen in burrows made by other animals and also in rock crevices. It is an extremely fast predator that goes after its prey with lightening fast speed once he has seen it. It then gives its prey a strong blow with its forelimbs.

It also has a complex set of eyes. Its eyes can even see ultraviolet light. It is extremely colourful. It can be 2-30 cms in length depending on the species.

112 Prawn

Prawn is found in calm and brackish waters across the globe. It also prefers warmer areas. It is often found on the sea floor and on the rocks. It is distinguished from the shrimp by the gill structure which is branching in prawns.

It prefers calm water so that it can make its nest there and then lays eggs. It feeds itself by filtering the nutritious particles out of the water flowing around it. Like other crustaceans it too has eight legs and two large powerful claws or pincers.

113 Shrimp

A Shrimp is a tiny animal that is found on the ocean floor in all the seas. There are about 2000 different species of shrimp. It has a hard and strong exoskeleton to support its body as it lacks a backbone. It can be about 23 cms in length. It is brightly coloured and has many pairs of legs. It often sheds its own shell as it grows in size.

It is an omnivore that eats both plants and small animals. It is a fast swimmer which uses its forelimbs to give a powerful blow to its prey. A shrimp can live for as long as five years.

CRUSTACEANS

114 Woodlice or Pill Bug

A Pill Bug or Woodlice is a crustacean whose body is divided into 14 parts. When threatened it can role itself into a tiny ball. It inhabits the damp and dark places in the forests and grasslands including staying among logs and dead leaves. It likes to stay in the soil where it gets plenty of moisture.

It is the only crustacean that does not lives in water. Like other crustaceans it sheds its outer shell as it grows in size. It is only a few centimetres long. It is a herbivore that eats plants and leaves.

115 Allosaurus

Allosaurus was probably the most powerful and fearsome dinosaur of the late Jurassic Period. Its name means 'different lizard', as its vertebrae is different from the other dinosaurs. It roamed earth during the late Jurassic Period about 150 million years ago.

It was a carnivore. Its jaws were huge and its teeth were long to tear apart meat. It had a powerful neck and head. Interestingly, when its teeth were shed, new grew in their place. It was about 40 feet in length. Its long, powerful legs helped it to gain speed and agility. Until the coming of the Tyrannosaurs, Allosaurus was the largest predator on earth.

116 Ankylosaurus

Ankylosaurus was an armoured dinosaur. It is also known as the 'fused lizard' and it lived on the North American continent during the late Cretaceous Period about 70-65 million years ago. It looked no less than a prehistoric tank.

It was a 30 feet long dinosaur that was covered with bony armoured plates from its head to its back. Its plates also had spikes on them. It even had a hammer or a club at the end of its tail. This slow moving dinosaur was a herbivore. It was among one of the heaviest dinosaurs.

117 Argentinosaurus

Argentinosaurus was one among the giant dinosaurs. It roamed the earth during the middle Cretaceous Period about 100-90 million years ago. Perhaps its giant size was a defence mechanism to help this herbivore survive against the meat eaters.

It was also among the heaviest dinosaurs. It was about 130 feet in length. Its fossils are huge though only a small part of them have been found in South America especially in Argentina. Based on these fossils, the dinosaur has been reconstructed.

118 Brachiosaurus

Brachiosaurus was a giant herbivore which had a stance similar to a modern giraffe. It lived during the late Jurassic Period about 150 million years ago. It is among the tallest dinosaurs that walked the earth. It lived in herds.

It was about 85 feet long with long front legs. It had chisel like teeth and its large nasal opening suggests that it may have a good sense of smell. It had equal number of teeth on its upper and lower jaws. It lived on the continents of Africa and North America.

DINOSAURS

119 Centrosaurus

Centrosaurus was a herbivore with a large horn on its head. It lived during the late Cretaceous Period about 75 million years ago. It usually lived in herds.

Its one forward-pointing horn was about 8 inches in length. It was its means of defence against its predators. Unlike others members of this species, it had poor defence. It also had a scalloped frill around its neck with hooked spikes near its centre. It was about 20 feet in length. It fed on low lying plants and its fossils have been found in Alberta in Canada.

120 Chasmosaurus

Chasmosaurus roamed the earth during the late Cretaceous Period around 75-70 million years ago. Its name Chasmosaurus means 'chasm lizard'. It is called so because of the holes in its frill.

This herbivore had a bulky body with horns. It was about 20 feet long with a long skull that also had a frill. Its frill was about 5 feet long. Its frill was rectangular in shape. Its face also had small horns. Its frill was not used as a means of defence but was for display purposes. It had a toothless beak.

121 Corythosaurus

Corythosaurus was called so because of his distinctive head crest. Its name means 'helmet lizard'. It lived during the late Cretaceous Period roughly about 75 million years ago.

Its head crest looked like a helmet. It was hollow and bony. It could be used to either make sounds, as a means to keep the head cool or perhaps it was merely for display during the courtship period. It was 30 feet long and was duck billed. This dinosaur was a herbivore. It was biped which means that it could walk comfortably either on two legs or on all four. Its fossils have been found in North America and Canada.

DINOSAURS

122 Deinonychus

Deinonychus is considered one of the deadliest dinosaurs that had roamed the earth though it was not a large dinosaur. Its name means 'terrible claw'. It lived during the middle Cretaceous Period about 100 million years ago.

It was a feared dinosaur because of its speed. It had large sickle like claws with which it ripped apart other dinosaurs. It went out to hunt in packs. Its slender tail had small bundles of bony rods. Its tail helped it to balance itself when it hunted or attacked its prey. It was quick and agile and was about 12 feet tall.

123 Dilophosaurus

Dilophosaurus was a carnivore with two bony crests on its head. It roamed the earth during the early Jurassic Period about 200-190 million years ago. Its bony crests were thin and hollow. The crests were almost circular and were perhaps used only for display.

It was lightly built for speed. It is estimated that this dinosaur may have moved in packs. Its bones were hollow. It was about 20 feet in length. Its neck was curved and shaped as an S. Its fossils have been found in China and the United States.

124 Diplodocus

Diplodocus, a herbivore, was among the longest land animals. It had an enormous neck and a long whip-like tail. It roamed the earth during the Jurassic Period about 156-145 million years ago.

Diplodocus had a unique body construction. On the underside of its tail, it had two rows of bones which provided this huge dinosaur extra support and greater mobility. It grew to be 90 feet in length. Its huge neck was 26 feet long and its whiplike tail was 45 feet long! This giant had a tiny brain. It is believed that it must have travelled in herds. It is also thought that its whip like tail must have made a crackling sound.

DINOSAURS

125 Giganotosaurus

Giganotosaurus, as the name suggests, was a giant dinosaur. It was a carnivore and was bigger than Tyrannosaurus Rex. It lived about 95 million years ago during the late Cretaceous Period. Its name, giga-noto-saurus means 'giant southern reptile'.

This huge meat eater was about 13-15 feet tall. It walked on two powerful legs and had bigger arms with three claws on it as compared to a T-rex. It had an enormous jaw that could have gulped down a human in one single bite! Its jaw was as big as an adult human being! This giant had a small brain.

126 Iguanodon

Iguanodon is among the most well-known dinosaurs. This herbivore is among those dinosaurs that had lived on every continent and were successful in surviving various climates. It spread to all the continents when the super continent Pangaea broke up. It lived during the early Cretaceous Period about 135-125 million years ago.

This huge herbivore was about 30 feet long. It was heavier than a modern day elephant. It looked scary with its foot long spikes at the end of its thumbs. Its spikes were a means to defend itself against predators. It was capable of moving on either two or four legs.

127 Kentrosaurus

Kentrosaurus was a herbivore dinosaur. Kentrosaurus means a 'spiked lizard'. It was called so because it had plates and spikes all over its body. This dinosaur had a walnut sized brain. It roamed the earth during the late Jurassic Period about 156-150 million years ago.

It measured to be 17 feet in length. It had a long and narrow skull with a toothless beak. Two rows of bony plates went from its neck to the mid section and to its tail. Two long spikes also provided protection to its shoulders. It ate low lying plants and it is believed that it kept its head low. It is also thought that it could move its spiked tail at dizzing speeds when it needed to protect itself from a predator.

128 Lambeosaurus

Lambeosaurus was a herbivore with a bony crest on its head. It is called Lambeosaurus after the Canadian fossil hunter Lawrence Lambe. It roamed the earth during the late Cretaceous Period about 83-65 million years ago.

It had a bill like a duck and it had a hollow, bony crest on its head. It must have been used to produce sounds or to signal other Lambeosaurus' that predators are near by. The crests of the males were larger than those of the females. It grew to 30-50 feet long. It had a keen eyesight and a good ability to hear. Its fingers were webbed. Fossilised skin and hand prints of Lambeosaurus have also been found.

DINOSAURS

DINOSAURS

129 Maiasaura

Maiasaura was a large herbivore whose fossils have been found in North America. Maiasaura means 'Good Mother Lizard'. It is called so because it is the first dinosaur species that showed that it cared for its young. It lived during the late Cretaceous Period around 80-65 million years ago.

Fossils of baby Maiasaura's show that the hatchlings were unable to walk due to their underdeveloped legs. They also had partially worn teeth showing that the adults fed them. Maiasaura's were about 30 feet long and had a muscular tail. Each of its eyes had a bony crest over them. These dinosaurs lived in large groups with about 10,000 beings in one herd. With many young ones with them, they protected their territory fiercely.

130 Mamenchisaurus

Mamenchisaurus was another huge dinosaur with a very long neck. Interestingly, it had the second largest neck of a known dinosaur! It lived during the late Jurassic Period about 156-145 million years ago.

This herbivore also had a very long tail. It grew to about 70-80 feet in length. It neck was 46 feet long with a 45 feet long tail. It is belived that it must have swung its long neck as it fed itself from tree to tree closer to the ground. It is thought so because it would have been difficult to pump blood to its head if it kept it vertical. It could easily reach a fourth floor window when standing tall!

131 Nodosaurus

Nodosaurus was a herbivore that was probably the most armoured dinosaur. It is often called a tank-like dinosaur. Nodosaurus means a 'knobby or node lizard'. It is called so because it had lumps and knobs all over its body. It lived during the late Cretaceous Period about 113-98 million years ago.

It was a quadrupedal and grew to about 13-20 feet in length. Its lumps and knobs gave it protection from the predator. Its tail, however, had no knobs or lumps on it. It fed on low-lying plants. No complete fossil of Nodosaurus have been found till date. It had a small head and a still smaller brain.

132 Ouranosaurus

Ouranosaurus was a herbivore dinosaur that had a sail on its back. It lived in a warm and dry climate. It roamed the African continent about 115-110 million years ago during the early Cretaceous Period. Its name Ouranosaurus means a 'brave lizard'.

Ouranosaurus had long spines sticking out of its backbone. This spine which formed a sail was covered with skin. These spines started from its back and went all the way to its tail. Its spine was a means to regulate temperature in the hot African sun. It grew to about 24 feet long. It had a short and flexible neck. Its sail could also have made it look larger to its predators.

DINOSAURS

133 Pentaceratops

Pentaceratops was a herbivore dinosaur that had a massive frill. It is also called a rhinoceros like dinosaur. It lived during the late Cretaceous Period about 75-65 million years ago. It is the record holder for having the largest skull of any land animal!

Pentaceratops had three horns on its face. A large bony plate, also known as a frill, extended from its head. Most of its skull is made up of its massive frill. It grew up to be 28 feet in length. It had a parrot like beak and two horn-like cheek bones that protruded from its face. It roamed constantly in search of food so that it could get nourishment from the food that it ate.

134 Sauropelta

Sauropelta was another armoured herbivore. Its name Sauropelta means a 'Lizard shield'. It is called so because its body too was covered with sharp spikes and plates. It roamed the earth during the early Cretaceous Period about 116-91 million years ago.

Its body was well armoured with sharp spikes and plates. It had a short neck and a stiff tail. Its tail had no plate or spikes. Sharp spikes also projected from near its neck to protect the neck from the jaws of the predators. It grew to about 19 feet in length. Its spikes must have made it look dangerous and bigger to its predators.

135 Spinosaurus

Spinosaurus was a carnivore. Its name means a 'spiny lizard'. It is called so because spines came out of its backbone to form a sail. It lived during the middle Cretaceous Period about 95 million years ago.

Spinosaurs grew to about 40-50 feet in length. It walked on two powerfully built legs. It was a carnivore with strong and powerful jaws with razor sharp teeth. Its lower jaw resembled that of the modern day crocodile. Its sail like spines helped it to regulate its body temperature in the warm and dry climate of Africa. The presence of a sail shows that it was a cold blooded animal that needed sun's warmth to regulate its body functions.

136 Stegosaurus

Stegosaurus was a large plant eating dinosaur that had two rows of huge plates running along its back. The name Stegosaurus means 'covered or roofed lizard'. It lived during the late Jurassic Period about 156-140 million years ago.

Stegosaurus grew to be about 26-30 feet in length. It had two rows of 17 huge plates each running from its back to its tail. The plates rose from its skin rather than being attached to its backbone. The largest of these plates were 60 cm tall and equally wide. Sharp spikes also protruded from its tail. It had a small brain which was the size of a walnut. The function of these plates could have been to regulate body temperature or to defend this herbivore dinosaur from its predators.

DINOSAURS

81

137 Thecodontosaurus

Thecodontosaurus is considered a very early dinosaur. It roamed the earth during the late Triassic Period. It lived when the earth was warm and much of the land was desert like.

It was a herbivore that grew up to 7 feet in length. Scientists believe that these dinosaurs could have been the earliest ancestors of the long necked dinosaurs of the sauropod family. It had a short head, a short neck and long legs. It probably ran on four legs but used its four legs to stand when grazing. Interestingly, its blunt teeth with serrated edges resemble the teeth of the monitor lizard!

138 Troodon

Troodon was a carnivore dinosaur. It is considerd one of the smartest dinosaurs due to its highly advanced brain. It roamed the North American continent during the late Cretaceous Period about 74-65 million years ago.

Troodon was a small dinosaur and was about 5 feet in length. It had a large head compared to its small size. It had forward looking eyes that provided it with better vision, even at night. It had razor sharp, curved teeth. It is therefore called Troodon which means 'wounded tooth.' It laid eggs at intervals and warmed them by sitting until the hatchlings hatched.

139 Tyrannosaurus Rex

Tyrannosaurus Rex is undoubtedly the most famous dinosaur. It is the largest carnivore that had lived on earth. It roamed the earth during the late Cretaceous Period. It went extinct about 65 million years ago.

It grew to be about 40 feet in length. It stood between 15-20 feet tall on its powerful, massive thighs. It also had a powerful tail that helped it to move. It had powerful jaws with sharp teeth which were replaceable. Its teeth were about 30 cm long! It also had tiny arms with two fingers. Its eyes were pointed towards the front that made it easier for this huge carnivore to find its prey. It could eat 230 gms of meat in one bite!

DINOSAURS

140 Ultrasaurus

Ultrasaurus was among the largest dinosaurs to roam the earth. It was a herbivore that had a giraffe-like stance. This giant dinosaur lived during the late Jurassic Period. Its name simply means an 'ultra lizard'.

This enormous dinosaur had longer front legs compared to its hind legs. It had a long neck and a small tail. It is thought to be more than 100 feet in length! When standing on all fours, Ultrasaurus could look inside a fifth or sixth floor window easily. If walking back to back, three Ultrasaurus could have covered the whole block! It was also twice as heavy as the other sauropods.

141 Utahraptor

Utahraptor was a dinosaur whose fossils have been found in the Cedar Mountain Formation in Utah and hence its name. It was a carnivore. It roamed the earth during the early Cretaceous Period about 132-119 million years ago.

It grew to be about 23 feet in length. It is known for its huge, distinctive claw on its hind feet. This claw was probably used to slash and tear at the prey. It had large, sharp eyes and gripping hands. It had a large brain. It was a fast runner on two slender, bird-like legs. This predator could have even hunted a large dinosaur when it hunted in packs.

142 Velociraptor

Velociraptor is another famous dinosaur. Its name Velociraptor means 'swift seizer'. Unlike its considered large size, it was relatively small. It was relatively about the size of a modern day turkey. It roamed the earth about 70 million years ago during the Cretaceous Period.

This small but dangerous predator was covered in feathers and walked on two legs. The feathers must have helped the dinosaur to regulate its body temperature. It grew to about 6 feet in length. It was among the smartest dinosaurs. It had a long claw on its feet and many razor sharp teeth in its mouth. It was a fast runner and could have ran at an estimated 37 mph.

DINOSAURS

EXTINCT ANIMALS

143 Archelon

Archelon was a giant turtle that swam the seas during the Cretaceous Period about 65-146 million years ago. It was a slow moving creature and was about 12 feet long. It had a sharp beak and large flippers that helped it to swim for long distances.

Unlike today's turtles, it did not have a hard shell. It instead had a skeletal structure. It also had flippers instead of arms and legs. It mostly swan on the sea surface to get its food—jellyfish and fish. Like many of today's turtles, it buried its eggs in sandy beaches. Leatherback Turtle is considered to be its closest relative.

144 Arsinoitherium

Arsinoitherium was a large mammal that resembled rhinoceros. It lived during the early Oligocene that is about 38-23 million years ago. Though similar in appearance to modern rhinoceros, it actually was related to the elephants.

It was a large quadruped that had a thick and hairless skin, a small brain and 5-toed feet. Its most distinguishing feature was its two huge, conical, hollow horns which were placed on its snout. Its horns were made of bones. It measured between 11-12 feet in length and was about 6 feet tall at the shoulder. It is assumed that it must have lived in groups near water. It was a herbivore. Its fossils have been found in Faiyum, Egypt.

145 Cryptoclidus

Cryptoclidus was an aquatic reptile. It is thought be a medium sized plesiosaur. It lived during the Jurassic Period around 165-159 million years ago. Its name means 'hidden collar bone.'

It measured about 13 feet in length. Its neck was 2 meters long. It had curved and interlocked teeth, a wide skull and huge paddle like flippers. It swam in shallow waters of the sea. It fed on small fish, shrimps and squid. Its fossils have been found in England, France and even in South America.

146 Desmatosuchus

Desmatosuchus was a huge armoured aetosaur. It ruled the earth during the Triassic Period around 230 million years ago. It was a reptile and not a dinosaur. It had spines running all along its length. It measured about 15-16 feet in length.

Among its many spines, two long spines jutted out from its shoulders. It had a bulky body with short legs and a small tail. The spines in its armour were as long as 18 cms. It was a herbivore. It had a short snout. Its fossils have been found in North America.

EXTINCT ANIMALS

EXTINCT ANIMALS

147 Dodo

Dodo in Portuguese means 'simpleton'. Dodo, a small bird was first seen in 1500s on the island of Mauritius. It was a flightless bird and is now extinct as a result of huntings.

It was bigger than a turkey but was related to the pigeons. It had a big head with a 9 inch long black bill tipped with red and its plumage was of blue-grey colour. It had small wings that were useless for flying. It had no known predators on the island until humans arrived. There are no complete specimens of Dodo.

148 Dunkleosteus

Dunkleosteus was an ancient fish that lived about 360 million years ago during the Late Devonian Period. It was a heavily armoured fish and had a shark like tail. It was a top predator and measured up to 11.5 feet.

It had no teeth. It instead had a large, scissor like cutting jaws which had razor sharp bones. Its body was scaleless and there were armour plates around its body. It was a carnivore that swam in the shallow waters of the world's seas. When food was scarce these fish also used to eat each other. Its fossils have been found widely distributed all across the globe.

149 Ekaltadeta

Ekaltadeta was a giant rat-kangaroo that inhabited the Australian continent. The word Ekaltadeta means 'powerful tooth'. It was a large marsupial that roamed the earth during the late Oligocene Period between 25-50 million years ago.

Its teeth were long, pointed forwards and were dagger like. It was a carnivore. It was as large as a wallaby though it was too big for rat kangaroos. It was probably an opportunistic carnivore. Its fossils only include skulls.

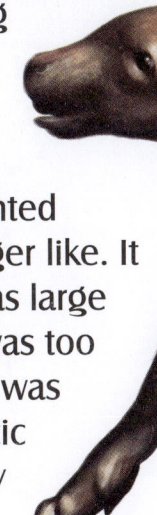

150 Elasmosaurus

Elasmosaurus was a marine reptile with a very long-neck. Its neck had 74-78 vertebrae. It roamed the seas during the late Cretaceous Period. It became extinct during the K-T mass extinction about 65 million years ago.

It was 45 feet in length. It had four paddle like flippers, a small head, sharp teeth and a pointed tail. It came on the surface to breathe air. It swam slowly through the seas like modern turtles and ate fish and shellfish. Its fossils have been found in North America. It is estimated that it must have come to the shore to lay its eggs.

EXTINCT ANIMALS

EXTINCT ANIMALS

151 Elephant Bird

Elephant Bird was native to the island of Madagascar. It was the largest bird that ever lived. It is called so not because it looked like an elephant but because it was big enough to seize a baby elephant.

It was a flightless bird that grew up to be 10-12 feet tall. It had long legs and feet with talons. Its neck too was powerful. It was a herbivore. It went extinct during the 16-17th centuries due to human intervention. Before it became extinct the bird had survived for 60 million years.

152 Eohippus

Eohippus, which means 'dawn horse', is the earliest known horse. It is also called Hyracotherium. It was the size of a small dog. It lived during the early Eocene Epoch about 50 million years ago. It inhabited the woodlands of North America and Western Europe.

It measured 2 feet in length. It had four toes on his front feet and three toes on its hind feet. It looked more like a small deer than a horse. This herbivore grazed soft leaves and plant shoots of low lying plants. The fossils of this ancient horse were first discovered in 1841.

153 Giant Moa

Moa or the Giant Moa was native to New Zealand. It inhabited New Zealand about 60 million years ago. Devoid of any predators on the island, Moa had no natural defences.

It grew to be 12 feet tall. It had a long neck and thick legs. It probably had a good sense of smell as is exhibited by its well developed nostrils. It had a small head which had small eyes. It became extinct with the coming of men in around 10th century in New Zealand.

154 Keichousaurus

Keichousaurus was among the oldest marine reptiles. It lived during the Triassic Period about 245-208 million years ago. It lived in the lakes and rivers of Asia. It is thought that it spent most of its time in water but may have come to land.

It was 15-30 cms in length. It had a long neck with a five toed feet. It had a pointed head and had sharp teeth. Its complete fossils have been found in China's Guizhou Province. It is because of its small size that its complete fossils have been found embedded in rocks.

EXTINCT ANIMALS

EXTINCT ANIMALS

155 Macrauchenia

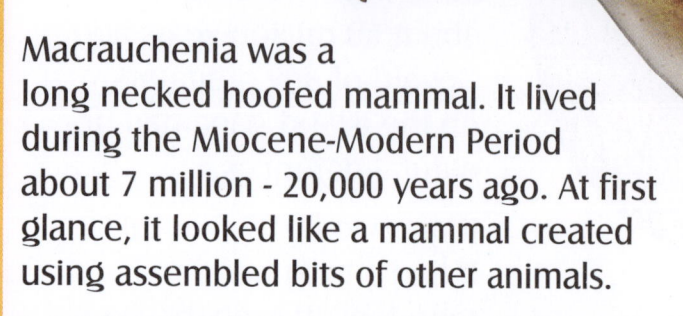

Macrauchenia was a long necked hoofed mammal. It lived during the Miocene-Modern Period about 7 million - 20,000 years ago. At first glance, it looked like a mammal created using assembled bits of other animals.

It had long thin legs that looked like that of a horse or camel, its long neck resembled that of a giraffe and its prehensile snout looked like a tiny elephant trunk. It was about 10 feet in length. It was a herbivore. Its fossils have been found in Argentina.

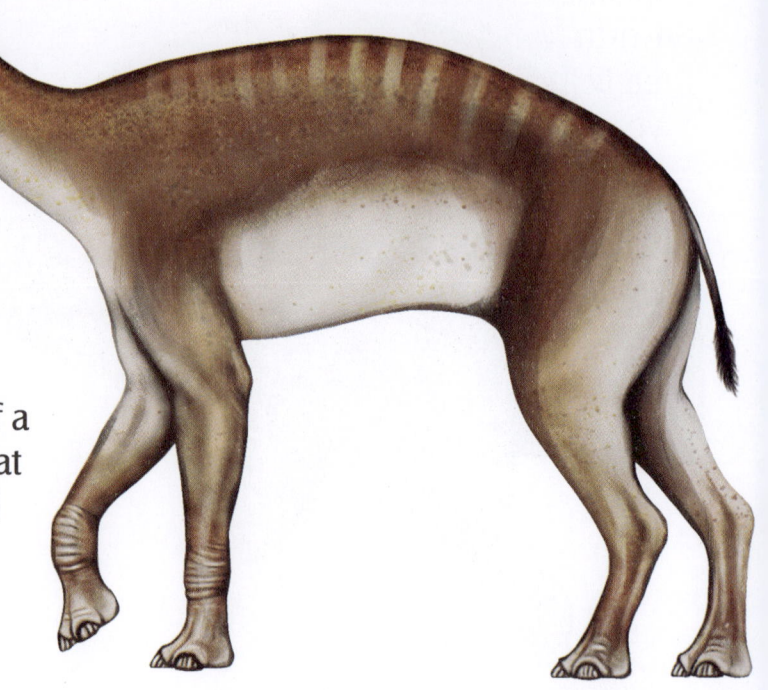

156 Megalodon

Megalodon was the descendant of today's Great White Shark. It lived about 25-1.6 million years ago during the Miocene and Pliocene epochs in the world's seas. This ancient predator grew to be about 40 feet in length. These estimates are a result of the fossilised teeth and vertebrae of the animal that have been found.

This giant's teeth were about 7 inches long! Like the Great White Shark, its teeth were arranged in rows. Its teeth have been found all over the world. It was a carnivore that fed on whales.

157 Morganucodon

Morganucodon was a small mammal. It inhabited the forests of Europe, Asia and North America during the late Triassic and early Jurassic Periods about 200 million years ago.

It was a tiny quadruped with five toes and a small tail. It was only four inches in length. It had large eyes and a narrow snout. It had a small brain. It was, however, very sensitive to higher frequencies. Its fossils have been found in Europe and also in China. Its large eyes indicate that it was perhaps nocturnal. It fed on insects and other small mammals.

158 Mosasaur

Mosasaurs were serpent like marine lizards. It was not a dinosaur but was related to semi-aquatic Aigialosaurs. It inhabited the warm seas during the late Cretaceous Period, the same time as the famous Tyrannosaurus Rex.

It was a powerful swimmer and grew up to be 17 metre long. It was a ferocious predator. It also came to the surface of the water to breathe air. Its fossils have been found all over the world. Its first fossils have been found in a limestone quarry in 1764. It fed on large fish, jelly fish and sometimes sharks.

EXTINCT ANIMALS

EXTINCT ANIMALS

159 Nothosaur

Nothosaurs were reptiles with a long neck and a long tail. They inhabited the world's seas during the Triassic Period about 250-210 million years ago. Though it came to the water surface to breathe air, it spent most of its time in water. It is known as the earliest reptilian sea hunters.

It grew up to about 10 feet in length. It had four wide, paddle-like limbs with webbed fingers and toes. Its long head had many sharp teeth. It also had nostrils at the end of its snout which indicated that it breathed air.

Its fossils have been found all over the world. It is assumed that it laid its eggs on land though it lived in the sea. It fed on fish and shrimp.

160 Orthacanthus

Orthacanthu was a freshwater shark. It lived during the Devonian-Triassic Period about 400-260 million years ago. It inhabited the earth before the dinosaurs.

Its most distinguishing feature was a spine that grew at the back of its skull. Its dorsal fin also stretched all along its back. It measured about 10 feet in length. Like other sharks, its teeth were arranged in rows. Its teeth were V shaped and razor sharp. Its body was sleek and hydrodynamic. This carnivore probably fed on fish and crustaceans.

161 Passenger Pigeon

Passenger Pigeons were once the most numerous birds on the planet. At the beginning of the 19th century their population was about 4 billion! With such numbers when their flocks travelled, they were many miles wide and several hundred miles long. Its habitat included North America.

However, due to loss of habitat and hunting made this bird go extinct. It had a blue head and rump, slate grey or black and a red wine breast. It had a small bill and scarlet eyes. It had long and slender wings. It could fly up to 60-70 miles an hour. The last Passenger Pigeon, named Martha, died alone at the Cincinnati Zoo on September 1, 1914.

162 Postosuchus

Postosuchus lived during the late Triassic Period about 222-215 million years ago. It was a fast running reptile and the topmost predator in southern United States. It was not a dinosaur but an ancestor of the present day crocodiles.

It grew to be 5 metres in length. It had a long tail, a broad skull and a narrow snout with numerous dagger like teeth. Its hind limbs were bigger than its front limbs. It had a five toed clawed feet. Long plates ran across its back. It was a carnivore. Its fossils have been found in Texas and also in Arizona.

EXTINCT ANIMALS

EXTINCT ANIMALS

163 Quagga

Quagga was native to the dry grasslands of South Africa. It became extinct in the 1880s. It was a large, hoofed mammal similar to Zebra. It was hunted for its meat and hide. The last Quagga, a female died in Amsterdam Zoo on August 12, 1883.

It was related to the zebras. It was called so because of its warning cry which went "Kwa-ha-ha". It had a yellowish-brown fur coat with stripes on its head, neck and chest. Its large eyes and ears helped it to detect its predators. It ran fast due to its long legs. It stood at around 53 inches at the shoulder. This herbivore lived in herds that consisted of a male, several females and the young ones. It spent most of its time in grazing grass. It was nomadic in nature.

164 Smilodon

Smilodon was a ferocious cat. It was the largest saber-toothed cat in the world. Though often mistaken for a tiger, it was a cat. It lived during the Pliocene-Modern Period about 5 million-10,000 years ago. It lived during the earth's last Ice Age. It inhabited North and South America.

It was 6 feet in length. Its most distinctive features were its huge canines which grew to 12 inches in length. It was a fierce predator. It was shorter than the lion but much heavier. It had short legs and a short tail. This carnivore sprang upon its prey with its powerful front legs. It wasn't a fast runner.

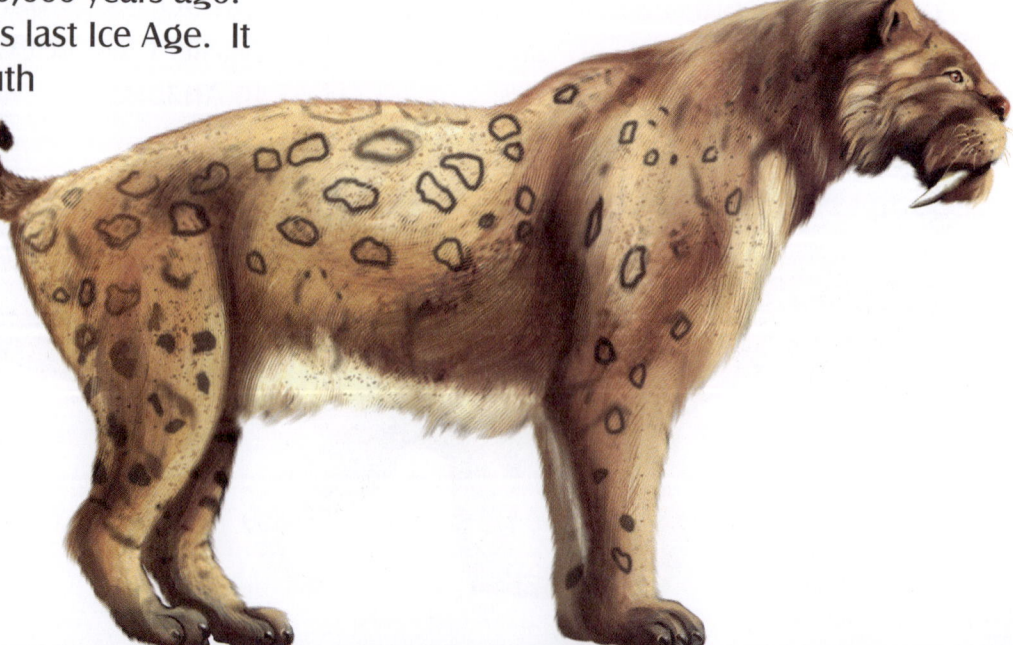

165 Tasmanian Tiger

The Tasmanian Tiger also called the Tasmanian Wolf and Thylacine was a carnivorous marsupial. It inhabited the forests and woodlands of Australia and Tasmania. It went extinct in Australia 2000 years ago and in Tasmania in 1936.

It had black to brown stripes on its back and tail. It was about 6 feet in length. It had grey or yellow to brown coat. It had a large skull and could open its jaws at 120 degrees more than any other animal. It had a wolf like head. It was a carnivore that hunted at night. It had a keen sense of smell and it pursued its victim until the prey was exhausted. The last known Tasmanian Tiger died in captivity at the Hobart Zoo.

166 The Great Auk

The Great Auk was related to Puffin. It was found around the Arctic Circle, Iceland and Greenland. It was a large flightless bird. It went extinct near 1841. It was mostly found in the rocky islands of the North Atlantic.

It was approximately 30 inches long with small wings. It used its small wings to swim underwater where they proved to be very useful. It had a large black bill that had eight or more transverse grooves. It had a white front like the penguins. It was killed as a food source and also its eggs were stolen and transported the world over. In 1844, the last known pair of The Great Auk and its egg were taken to Iceland.

167 Woolly Mammoth

Woolly Mammoths, often seen in cave paintings, were large elephants that inhabited earth during the last Ice Age. It lived about 120,000-4,000 years ago. It had a long, black thick fur and two huge curving tusks.

It grew to about 11.5 feet. Its tusks, which could grow to 15 feet, were its biggest distinguishing feature. Besides its thick coat of fur, it also had a four inch layer of fat beneath its skin to protect it against the cold. Its ears were small. It used its tusks to dig ground, to find food and also to defend itself. It was hunted by the early humans and they along with the warming climate may have led to its extinction. It was closely related to the Indian elephant.

168 Angelfish

Angelfish are found both in warm waters and also in freshwaters. It is a brightly coloured fish that is found in coral reefs and also in shallow subtropical waters. There are about 100 different species of Angelfish.

Angelfishes are brightly coloured. Its colours vary from blue, yellow and green to black. It is from 3-12 inches long. The triangular shape of the freshwater Angelfish allows it to hide itself more efficiently among the corals. It feeds on smaller fish, shrimps and algae found in the coral reefs.

FISH

169 Archerfishes

Archerfish are unique because of their peculiar way of hunting insects and other small terrestrial animals from branches hanging above the water. It hunts by firing with great accuracy streams of water into the air on their prey, knocking down animals as big as small lizards onto the water's surface. Once the prey has fallen into the water, the fish dashes and gulps its prey. The fish can shoot water upto 4m.

170 Basking Shark

The Basking Shark is found in all the oceans of the world except the Indian Ocean. It is the second largest shark in the world. It is also called 'sunfish' as it keeps close to the sea surface. It can grow to about 30 feet long in length.

It is a filter feeder shark. It is also known for its huge mouth that opens up like a balloon. As it opens its mouth, water comes in along with the tiny planktons in the water. It eats the planktons and small fish while the water is drained out. It slowly swims in the water, moving its entire body from side to side unlike other sharks that move using their tails.

171 Bluefin Tuna

Bluefin Tuna is the largest tuna. It is a fast moving fish. Its body is torpedo shaped, streamlined and is made for speed. it is found in the Atlantic and is also a much sought after fish in the Mediterranean Sea.

Bluefin Tuna is metallic blue in colour and is shimmering white at the bottom. It can grow up to 6-8 feet long. It eats fish, including Mackerel. It shoots out of the water at 43 miles an hour. It is also known for its yearly migration from the American to European waters. Interestingly, the Atlantic Bluefin Tunas are warm blooded and are also comfortable in cold waters.

172 Bony Fish

Bony Fish are found all over the world. It is found in a variety of colours and shapes and sizes. What makes these fish stand out is the fact that it has a skeleton made of bones whereas many fish have a skeleton made of cartilage. A Bony Fish also has a hard plate covering its gills, a swim bladder and has bony plate like scales on its body.

Bony Fish may vary from 0.5 inches to 15 feet. A Bony Fish feeds on planktons, small fishes and crustaceans. Salmon, eels, catfish and sea horses are some of the Bony Fish.

FISH

173 Clown Fish

Clown Fish are found in the shallow waters of the Indian Ocean, the Red Sea and also in the Pacific Ocean. It is a brightly coloured small fish that lives among anemone. Anemone is a sea creature with poisonous tentacles that looks like a flower and feeds on small fish.

A Clown Fish has a bright orange skin with three white stripes. It is about 11 cms in length. It is mostly found living in the corals. A layer of mucus on the Clown Fish skin makes it immune to the sting of the anemone. The Clown Fish in exchange of the protection it gets from the anemone, helps its host by cleansing it.

174 Coelacanth

Coelacanth was long thought to be extinct until it was discovered in 1938 in the Indian Ocean. It is a primitive fish meaning that it had been there since the time of the dinosaurs. It is therefore also called a 'living fossil'.

Its most distinctive feature includes a pair of lobe fins that extend from its body like legs. It also has a hinged joint in its skull which allows it to open its mouth very wide for a large prey. It inhabits the deep sea partly due to its sensitive eyes and can grow up to 6-7 feet in length.

175 Deep Sea Angler Fish

Angler Fish are found deep in the sea. It has a bizarre and distorted appearance. It inhabits the depths of the Atlantic and the Antarctic Oceans. It is generally dark grey or brown in colour.

It has a large head with many sharp, translucent teeth in its crescent shaped mouth. It gets its name from a piece of dorsal spine that protrudes over its mouth like a fishing pole. At the end of it is a piece of luminous flesh that helps it to catch its prey deep down. Its mouth is so wide and its body is so flexible that it can easily fit a larger prey in its mouth. Only female Angler Fish have this characteristic.

The male Angler Fish is very small compared to the female and is dependent on the female for its survival.

176 Electric Eel

The Electric Eel is a long fish that produces electricity. It can produce a 600 volt electric shock that is enough to stun its prey. Repeated shocks can even kill its prey including humans. It is found in the freshwaters of the Amazon Basin and the Orinoco Basins in South America.

It can grow up to be 6-8 feet long. The electricity producing organs are located in its abdomen. It lives in the muddy waters of the basins. It has poor eyesight. It can, however, emit a low charge that acts as a radar allowing it to navigate and locate its prey.

FISH

FISH

177 Goldfish

Goldfish is the most domesticated fish in the world. It is a freshwater fish. It is a small member of the carp family. It varies in colour, size and shape. Mostly it is golden-orange in colour but it can also be black, green or white in colour.

It eats aquatic plants and insects. It has two sets of paired fins-pectoral and pelvic fins. It has large eyes and acute sense of hearing and smell. It can grow to be 3-5 inches long. It is found in aquariums around the world.

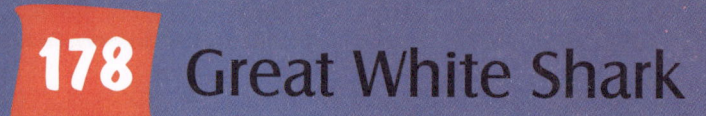

178 Great White Shark

Great White Shark is the largest predator in the seas. It is found in the cool waters across the globe. It can grow to 15 feet in length. It has a torpedo shaped body with a mouth that has about 3,000 teeth at any one time.

It has a powerful tail that can propel it through the water at a speed of 15 miles per hour. Its teeth are arranged in several rows in its mouth. It has a grey coloured upper body while its underbelly is white. Its skeletons are made of cartilage. Its liver is big and oily which helps it float. It hunts sea lions, small whales, sea turtles and sometimes even carrion.

179 Gulper Eel

The Gulper Eel is a long eel that inhabits the depths of the seas. It has a huge mouth with tiny teeth. It opens its mouth wide to eat or gulp down its prey. It inhabits the warm temperate waters of the Atlantic, Pacific and the Indian Oceans.

It is about two feet long. It has a long stomach and small eyes. Its spineless fins are joined all across its body. It has tiny scales covering its body. It feeds on small fish, shrimp and plankton.

FISH

180 Hatchetfish

Hatchetfish inhabit the warm and temperate water all across the globe. It is a small fish with shiny scales. It usually swims in the depths of the sea. It, however, is also found in freshwaters.

It has an odd shaped body. It has a flattened body with a wing shaped pectoral fins. It uses the pectoral fins to jump out of water. It has large eyes and small light organs on the underside of its body. It can be as long as 10 cms. It feeds on insects and their larvae. It is also one of the fish that are kept as pets.

FISH

181 John Dory

John Dory are found around New Zealand. It inhabits the mid waters and the ocean floor. It is an olive coloured fish with a black spot. It is a weak swimmer and therefore it does not survive in the deep sea.

It is about 2 feet long on an average. It has long distinctive spines coming out of its dorsal fin. It has a smooth skin with tiny scales. It has a flattened body. It can be very difficult to spot as the spines on its body are motionless. It is among a widely eaten fish.

182 Lake Trout

Lake Trout is a freshwater fish that is found in Alaska and Canada. It is a fast moving and the largest freshwater fish. It has a silvery body with pale spots on its head, back and sides.

Its body is torpedo shaped and it has a deeply forked tail. It has a large head with sharp teeth in its mouth. It can grow up to 1.2 m in length. It is a carnivore that feeds on shrimps, insects and smaller fish.

183 Lantern Fish

Lantern Fish are found all over the world. It inhabits depths of 200-1000 m. It has tiny lights also called photophores all over its body and hence its name. These tiny lights are located on its belly, tail and sometimes even around its eyes. It can even make the light appear bright or dim depending on its surroundings.

At night, it swims to shallow waters. It can be as long as 35cms. It has huge eyes. It mainly feeds on krill and on small invertebrates. These lights are also used as a means of communication.

184 Leafy Seadragon

Leafy Seadragons inhabit the warm temperate waters around the Australian continent. It is a small, well camouflaged creature. It is about 35 cms in length.

It has leaf-shaped extensions all over its body and hence its name. These extensions help it to blend in with the weeds easily and difficult for the predators to spot it. It has a long, thin snout with a slender body that is covered in bony rings. It also has a long tail. Like seahorses, the male seadragons bear the children. It eats sea lice and mysids.

185 Long-spined Porcupine Fish

A Long-spined Porcupine Fish inflates itself and fills itself with water when it gets threatened. It makes the spines on its body stand out. It thus becomes impossible for the predator to eat it.

It has a pale body with dark brown spots. It grows to 35 cms. The spines on its body lay flattened until it inflates itself. It has large eyes set in a big head. It inhabits almost all the seas of the world even along the coral reefs.

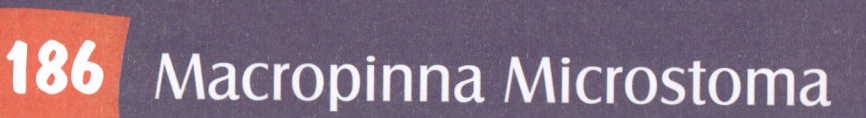

186 Macropinna Microstoma

Macropinna Microstoma is one of the weirdest fish of the world. It inhabits the deep waters of the North Pacific Ocean. It is normally found at 600-800 metres.

Its most striking feature is its transparent head that has its barrel like eyes. Its eyes are topped by green leaf-like lenses. Its eyes can be rotated to either look straight upwards or forward. This chamber is filled with a fluid. It is also called Barrel-eyed Fish. It can grow to be 15 cm long.

187 Manta Ray

Manta Rays inhabit the warm, tropical waters of the oceans across the globe. It is the largest ray. It can measure about 22 feet. It has a flat body and a small tail. Unlike some rays it does not have a stinging spine. It uses its pectoral fins gracefully to swim in the ocean.

Its small tail allows it to perform acrobatic skills and sometimes to leap out of the water surface. It does not have teeth and uses the tiny plates in its mouth to filter the food particles. Despite its size, the Manta Ray is hunted by many predators including the Great White Shark and the Killer Whale.

FISH

188 Mushroom Scorpionfish

Scorpionfish inhabits the temperate and tropical waters of the world. It is sometimes also called Stone Fish or a Rock Fish. It is so called because it is usually seen living among the rocks.

It has spines on its head and fins which are sometimes venomous. The venom can cause a painful wound. It has small feathery fins that allow it to camouflage itself with its surroundings. It lies quietly hidden at the sea bottom until its prey comes along. It is the most dominant predator in its surroundings.

FISH

189 Piranha

Piranha is found in the freshwaters across South America. It is also called Caribe. It has a single row of razor-sharp teeth. It hunts in groups called school. Depending on the various species it can be 15-60 cms long. It is known for its ferocity.

When any of its teeth gets broken, another one replaces it. It ranges in colour from steel grey to yellow to red and black. It has excellent hearing. It is a carnivore and feeds on birds, fish and aquatic plants and sometimes even on small mammals. It is usually seen in fast flowing rivers where there is plenty of food.

190 Pufferfish

Pufferfish with its many varieties are found in the warm, temperate waters around the world. Some species are even found in brackishwater and freshwater. It is also called Blowfish and Swellfish. When it is threatened it swells itself by gulping lots of water, making itself difficult to be eaten. But when it puffs itself, its swimming slows down.

Even if it finds its way into the predators mouth, it contains an enzyme called tetrodotoxin which makes it foul smelling and sometimes toxic for the predator.

It has a long body with a large head. It can be 3 feet in length. It does not have scales and its skin is usually rough.

191 Pupfish

Pupfish are native to the south-western United States. This fish is found in small ponds, lakes, springs and streams etc. It is a small fish that has adapted itself to live in harsh climates.

The Pupfish is endangered as most of the pools dry up during the summer season, killing many pupfish. During winters, it stays at the muddy bottoms of the lakes and streams until it is summer again.

Pupfish are tiny fish that come in a number of colours. It feeds on insects and invertebrates.

192 Red Lionfish

Red Lionfish is found in the shallow waters and the coral reefs of the Indian and west Pacific Oceans. It is a venomous fish with a bright red coloured body. It hunts just like the lions do and hence its name.

A Lionfish can be 1 foot long. It has a large head, unique rayed fins and venomous spines on its body. It uses camouflage and its fast reflexes when it hunts its prey. It usually preys on crabs, small fish and shrimps. Venom from one of its spines can be very painful and can cause breathing problems.

FISH

FISH

193 Salmon

Salmon inhabits almost all the waters of the world. It is an anadromous fish. It means that Salmon spends all their lives in the seas which are salty but they come to the freshwaters to reproduce. Its journey from the sea to freshwater can be hundreds of miles long. During this time, a Salmon does not eat and its colour changes too. It has a silvery skin with a spotted back. It is a carnivore.

When the salmon fry hatch from their eggs, they eat their egg yolk as their food source and later eat insects. After some time, they find their way to the sea on their own.

194 Seahorse

Seahorses inhabit the shallow temperate waters around the world. It is usually seen in coral reefs, mangrove forests and among sea grasses. It is a small fish, from a few centimetres to a foot long, with its body covered in armoured plates. It uses its small body and its colours to camouflage itself.

It is a shy creature with a head that resembles a horse and a curled tail. It is usually seen hanging to a branch or weed with the help of its curled tail. Interestingly, Sea Horses are the only animals where the father gets pregnant!

195 Stonefish

Stonefish is native to the shallow waters of Australia. It is called so because of its stone like appearance. Its appearance allows it to blend itself with its surroundings. It lies still on the ocean floor, waiting for its prey.

Along with its stony appearance, it has sharp spines on its back that are poisonous. It can be up to 35 cms long. It has a brownish appearance. It feeds on shrimp and small fish and when they are close enough, it opens its mouth with lightening speed to gulp them.

196 Sun Fish

Sun Fish also called Mola is found in warm and temperate waters. It is a silvery white, large fish. It is an unusual fish that has long pectoral and dorsal fins but its back fin does not grow. It instead gets folded and does the work of a rudder.

The Sun Fish is often seen basking in the sun, floating on its side. It is the heaviest bony fish in the world. It can grow to be 10-13 feet long. It has a circular appearance with large eyes and a small mouth. Often its rough skin gets invested by parasites so it invites small fish and birds to help it get rid of them.

FISH

FISH

197 Swordfish

Swordfish are found in almost all the waters of the world at depths of 400-500 metres. It is among the fastest moving fish in the seas at 60 mph. Its most distinctive feature is its extended upper jaw that appears like a sword and hence its name.

It can be between 7-15 feet in length. It migrates each year from its feeding grounds to spawning grounds. Swordfish is a carnivore. A Swordfish can lay thousands of eggs at a time. It has very few predators.

198 Whale Shark

Whale Shark is found in warm and tropical oceans around the world. It is a filter feeder and the world's largest fish. Though it has a large mouth, it feeds on plankton and small fish. It swims slowly with its mouth open and its food gets into its mouth which it filters from the water.

It can grow to 33 feet in length. Its large mouth can be as big as 5 feet and it has rows and rows of teeth. It has a flat head and its eyes are located on the front side of its face. It breathes through the gills and takes oxygen from the water.

199 Ant

Ants are found around the world in a variety of habitats. More than 10,000 species of Ants have been discovered around the world. Ants live in colonies. All the Ants in the colony are related to each other. A colony can consist of thousands of Ants.

A colony usually has a queen ant, who only lays eggs, worker and soldier ants that work, find food and defend the colony and male ants who only mate with the queen ant.

Ants are small insects measuring barely 0.8-1 inches. Its body is made of a head, thorax and an abdomen along with two antennae. Interestingly, ants can lift and carry things three times their size.

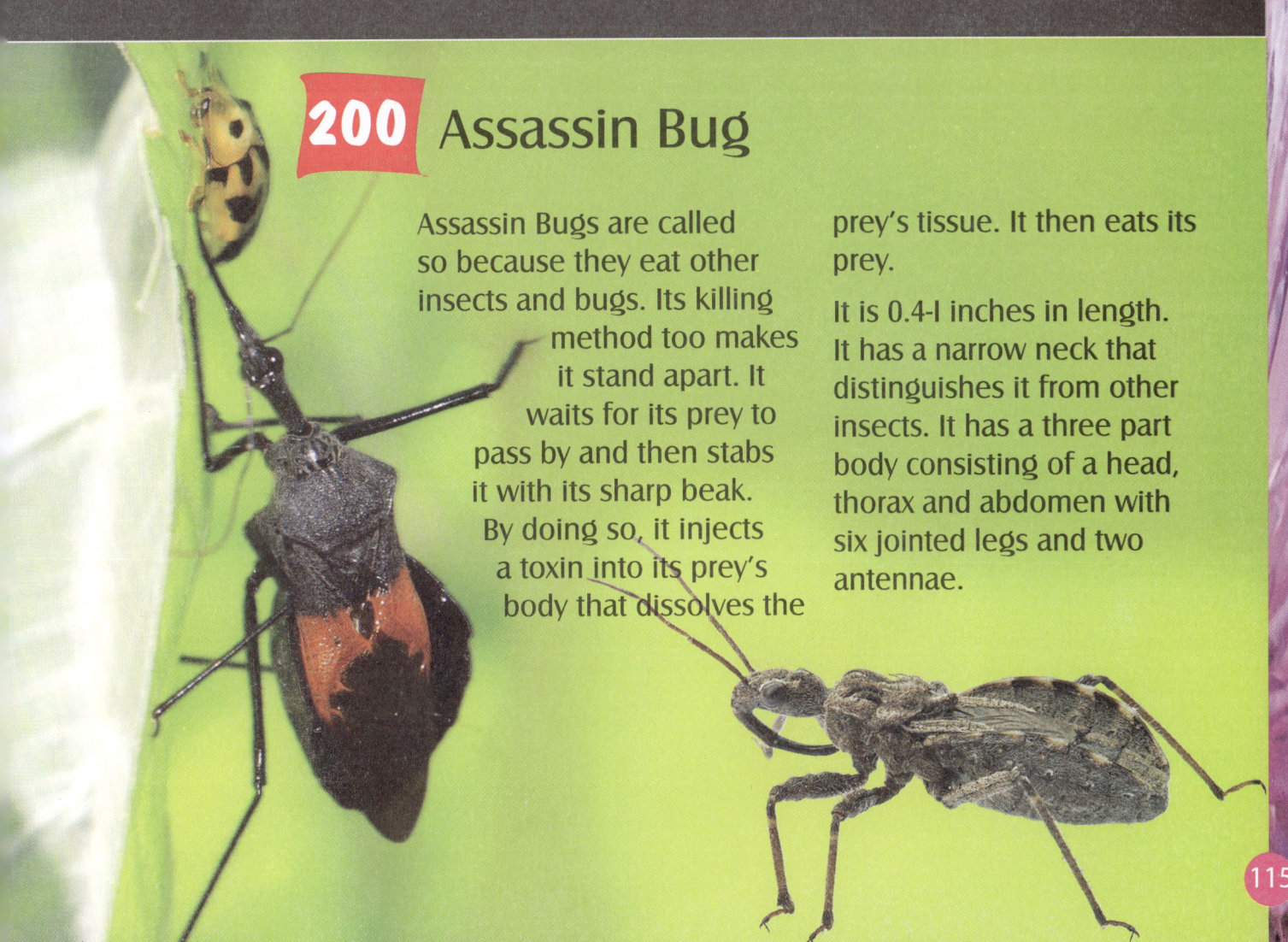

INSECTS

200 Assassin Bug

Assassin Bugs are called so because they eat other insects and bugs. Its killing method too makes it stand apart. It waits for its prey to pass by and then stabs it with its sharp beak. By doing so, it injects a toxin into its prey's body that dissolves the prey's tissue. It then eats its prey.

It is 0.4-1 inches in length. It has a narrow neck that distinguishes it from other insects. It has a three part body consisting of a head, thorax and abdomen with six jointed legs and two antennae.

INSECTS

201 Beetles

Beetles are easily distinguished by their shell like exterior. It is the largest order of the animal kingdom in the world. Like other insects, it too has a three part body consisting of a head, thorax and an abdomen. It is found around the world in all kinds of habitats including deserts, rainforests, rivers, mountains and cold climates.

Beetles are found in various shapes, colours and sizes. It has two sets of wings, one are leathery, protective wings and the other are wings used for flight. Its sizes vary from a few millimetres to a few inches long. The antennae on its head help it to find food and other beetles.

202 Blue Morpho Butterfly

Blue Morpho Butterfly is among the largest butterflies in the world. Its wingspan can be anywhere between five to eight inches. It is known for its bright blue wings which are bordered by black. It is native to the rainforests of South and Central America.

The underside of its wings is however a dull brown with many eye spots. The dull brown colour acts as a camouflage against its predators. It spends most of its time at the forest floor keeping its wings usually closed. Adults drink the juices of rotting fruits using their long proboscis. Its lifespan lasts for only 115 days.

203 Cicada

Cicadas are distributed around the world. It is a tiny insect with a dark coloured body with four long, transparent wings. It can be 0.7-2.25 inches in length. It is known for the loud sound it makes and which is picked up by the other cicadas. It is usually seen perched on trees.

It is the longest living insect in the world. Cicadas sounds though seem similar to us are distinct. The sound varies to communicate danger and also to attract mates. It is also known for disappearing for years. Some species of Cicada are however seen annually.

204 Crickets

Crickets are found all over the world. It is related to the grasshopper. It is found in all sorts of habitats including grasslands, fields, meadows and your backyard. It is known for the loud chirping sound made by the male crickets. It makes the sound by rubbing its forewings together. In warmer areas, the chirp of the crickets increases. It can be 0.12-2 inches in length. It has thin, long antennae and long, modified legs for jumping. It has highly sensitive organs on its forelegs which receive sound. It mostly comes out at night. It is also kept as pets as many people think that crickets bring good luck.

INSECTS

INSECTS

205 Dragonfly

Dragonfly is found all over the world near water. It is often seen hovering near swamps, ponds and lakes. It has a large, thin body and two pairs of transparent wings. It is brightly coloured.

While flying, it can propel itself into six directions. It can be 1-5 inches in length. It is a carnivore and eats smaller insects. Most of the species of dragonfly are found near water and it lays its eggs in water. Interestingly, it will fly only when it is warm. It is also one of the oldest insects on earth.

206 Firefly

Firefly or the lightening bug is found in warm climates of Asia and the Americas. It is distinguished by the glow it produces. It comes out at night.

It is a small winged insect. It prefers to stay in places where it is moist and humid. It is about 0.7 inches long. It is black in colour with yellow lines on its forehead. It can control, making it bright or dim, its glowing light. It inhales oxygen and with the help of a special substance called luciferin produces light. Though its light is bright it has no glow. Male fireflies flash the light every five seconds and the females flash the light every two seconds.

207 Grasshopper

Grasshoppers are found all over the world. It is seen in gardens, fields and forests. It can hop, walk and fly. It is known for jumping to great distances and heights. It too makes a chirping sound by rubbing its back legs together.

It is a herbivore. It can be as much as 5 inches in length. It has no ears to hear. It hears with the help of a organ in its abdomen called tympanal organ. It uses its back legs to hop. Interestingly, grasshoppers have 5 eyes. Two of its eyes are compound eyes.

INSECTS

208 Harlequin Bug

Harlequin Bug is found in the US and especially in Mexico. This insect is a pest. It is usually seen in cabbage fields. It is a small insect with a black coloured body with bright orange markings and wings. It can be 7-10 mm in length.

It hatches from a tiny, barrel shaped egg. Its eggs are yellow to grey with black bands and a black spot. The nymph (young ones) when they are born are a miniature of the adults though they have no wings. It feeds on plants. It pierces the leaves with its needle-like mouth and sucks out the sap. In doing so, it damages the plant.

INSECTS

209 Honey Bee

Honey Bees like ants are social animals. It lives in hives. It is found in warm climates all across the world. Honey Bees suck the nectar out of the flowers and turn it into honey in its hive.

It can fly at about 15 mph. As it goes from flower to flower collecting nectar, the pollens from the flowers get stuck to its hind legs. This pollen from one flower gets deposited on another flower. Through this process, the flowers get fertilized and it makes seeds.

A queen bee rules the hive while the worker bees collect nectar, make honey and also defend the hive. Interestingly, during winters, the bees depend on community warmth in order to stay alive.

210 Housefly

Housefly, a common insect, is found around the world. It lives in all kinds of habitats. It is merely 6-12.5 mm in length. It has a pair of transparent wings. A Housefly can also use its feet to taste. Interestingly, a Housefly cannot bite. It can only drink. It can, however, turn many solid things into liquid with its saliva.

It uses its antennae to smell and can fly upto 45 miles per hour. It can beat its wings 200 times per second. Interestingly, the Housefly is also a carrier of disease. Did you know that it has been on earth for a very long time!

211 Jumping Bean Moth

Jumping Bean Moth is found in Mexico especially in the deserts. It is a grey to brown coloured moth. It lays its eggs inside the flowers of the shrub *Sebastiana pavoniana* along with a few other plants. What distinguishes it apart is that when the moth is at the caterpillar stage, it lives inside a seed pod. And when the caterpillar moves inside the seed pod, so does the seed pod. The caterpillar jumps when it is exposed to heat and warmth. And it is due to this jumping pod that the insect gets its name.

212 Ladybug

Ladybug is found all over the world in grasslands, gardens, forests and in fields. It is a tiny insect belonging to the beetle family. It is red coloured, oval shaped insect with black spots. It is only 4-8 mm in length.

Ladybugs are voracious eaters. It eats the aphids which are plant eating insects. It is the reason that farmers are happy when they see ladybugs in their field. Its spots are also a warning to its predator saying that it would not taste good. It also produces a fluid which it releases from the joints in its legs that gives a foul taste when it is eaten. It also pretends to be dead when threatened by its predators.

INSECTS

213 Leafcutter Ant

Leafcutter Ants are native to South America and parts of North America. It lives in tropical forests. These ants grow their own food which is a fungus. It is a social ant which lives in large underground colonies. It can carry ten times its own weight.

It spends its time in searching leaves in the forest. It cuts the leaves from plants with its sharp jaws and carries them to its underground gardens where the leaves are chewed into a pulp. With time, fungus grows on the leaves and this fungus is its food. It also produces some enzymes and acids to help the fungus grow quickly along with enzymes that can check the fungal growth.

214 Mosquito

Mosquito, a common insect, is found around the world. It is more often found near a water source. It is a tiny insect with a pair of veined wings. It also has a straw like proboscis which helps it to suck liquids.

It sucks blood and nectar from plants. When it bites, it injects an anti clotting enzyme in the body of its prey. This enzyme does not allow the blood to stop flowing. It finds its victim by its sight, sense of smell and warmth.

The female mosquito is a carrier of disease like malaria and dengue. It is the female mosquito that sucks blood to provide proteins to its eggs. The males only drink nectar.

215 Pond Skater or Water Strider

Pond Skater or Water Strider is a tiny insect that can run across the water surface. It is found in most parts of Europe in streams and ponds. It uses its long middle legs like paddles to wade through the water. Its long hind legs help it to steer across the water. It rarely goes under the water.

It uses its short front legs to capture its prey. It also captures and feeds on insects that fall into the river. It is about 5 mm in length. Its body is covered in velvety hairs that prevent it from falling in water. During winters, it flies away to hibernate and returns to the water when the temperatures are warmer. It is sensitive to the vibrations on the water surface that also help it to locate its prey.

216 Praying Mantis

Praying Mantis is found on trees and bushes in warm climates. It is often seen in gardens as it eats the insects that are found there. It is called so because of its prominent bent front legs. Its legs are held at such an angle that it seems to be praying.

It is about 5-6 inches in length. It also uses its front legs to capture and hold its prey. It has powerful eyes that can see about 50-60 feet away. It camouflages itself among leaves as it hunts its food which is mostly insects. Interestingly, it can rotate its triangular shaped head to 180 degrees on either sides.

INSECTS

INSECTS

217 Silkworm

Silkworms are native to Northern China. Surprisingly, it is the caterpillar of a moth that weaves the silk. Hence, the weaver of the silk is not a worm at all.

The caterpillar weaves a cocoon of silk in which it stays until it becomes a pupa and finally emerges as a moth. The silk thread of cocoon is one single thread that can be 300-900 mm long. This thread is made of a protein which is secreted from two salivary glands which are located in the head of the caterpillar. Harvesting silk from the Silkworm was first started in China thousands of years back. Interestingly, the moth is unable to fly because of its small wings and a fat body.

218 Termite

Termites are tiny insects that are found in tropical and subtropical areas around the world. This tiny insect eats lots and lots of wood. It eats non stop all the time! Termites are found in dark, damp places. It is also found in tree stumps, logs and in the soil.

It is a social insect that lives in large colonies that may contain thousands of individuals. It requires moisture in order to survive. It is a light coloured insect whose forewings and hindwings lie flat on its back once it has found a suitable place to eat wood. Did you know that the total weight of all of the Termites in the world is more than the weight of all the humans in the world?

219 Walking Stick

The Walking Stick insect is a long insect that looks like a stick. It is usually seen on trees, grasslands or bushes. It is found in tropical and subtropical regions around the world. It is a herbivore that can camouflage itself completely. It is usually brown or green in colour.

It has 6 long legs and two long antennae. It walks slowly. It has a hard exoskeleton. It can be 0.46-12.9 inches long. Usually the females are longer than the males. It comes out mostly at night. It can shed its limbs if threatened by a predator. Later, it can regenerate the lost limb.

220 Wasp

Wasps are found around the world. It is a tiny insect with strong jaws, a narrow waist and a pair of wings to fly. Females of some species also have a stinger. It feeds on insects, spiders and also nectar. Though Wasps are feared by humans, it is actually helpful to humans as it gets rid of the pests.

Depending on the species, Wasps can be social or solitary. It makes its nest with chewed wood and plant fibres to lay its eggs. During winter, most Wasps die except the queen. The queen hibernates during the winter.

INSECTS

221 Yellow Jacket Wasp

Yellow Jacket Wasp is an easily recognizable wasp. It is a very aggressive wasp. The females have stringer which they do not hesitate to use against their victim. It is distinguished by its yellow and black colours.

It feeds on other insects in order to provide nutrients to its larvae. It is about 14-25 mm in length. It lives in colonies. The colonies may contain from a few hundred to a thousand individuals. It usually nests underground. It defends its nest very forcefully once it is disturbed.

INSECTS

222 Corals

Corals are organisms that build coral reefs. It lives in compact colonies which include thousands of individuals called 'polpys'. Polpys are tiny and soft body organisms with a hard limestone skeleton.

The moment a polpy attaches itself to a rock, it is the beginning of a reef. In no time the tiny polpy multiplies itself into hundreds and thousands of identical individuals. As the reef develops, it gets brightly coloured. Its bright colours are due to the large quantities of algae that live in the coral reefs.

Corals are highly sensitive to climate change. With a slight change in temperature, the corals become white and eventually die. Did you know that it is the only living structure that can be seen from space!

INVERTEBRATES

INVERTEBRATES

223 Jellyfish

Jellyfish are animals without bones. It is found in all the world's oceans. It is also called Jellies or Sea Jellies. Depending on the species, it can be seen inhabiting the ocean surface or the ocean depths.

It is a free swimming animal. It is often seen floating in large groups. Despite being called a fish, a jellyfish is not a fish. It has a soft body made of jelly and covered by a thin layer of skin. It has long, stinging tentacles which are used to catch its prey. Its body is made up of 90% water. Box Jelly is one of the deadliest jellies.

224 Octopus

Octopus, meaning eight footed, inhabits all the world's oceans. It is usually seen on the ocean floor. It can range from 12-36 inches depending on the species. It has eight arms with two rows of sucker pads on them.
It is a master of disguise.
It has an amazing ability to hide itself in plain sight by matching its texture, pattern and colour to its surroundings.
It can also release a cloud of black ink if the predator sees it. Further, it loses an arm to distract its predator. Interestingly, it can squeeze itself through the narrowest places. It is considered a highly intelligent animal.

225 Sea Anemone

Sea Anemone is found in all the world's oceans on the ocean floor. It is a colourful animal. It spends most of its time stuck to the rocks on the ocean floor. It has venom filled tentacles which it uses to catch unsuspecting fish.

It has a cylindrical body with tentacles that surround its mouth. At the slightest touch, the tentacles release a toxin that paralyses the prey. The prey then is consumed by the Sea Anemone. Sea Anemone can be from half an inch to 6 feet in length. Interestingly, the Clownfish are immune to its tentacles' sting.

226 Sea Cucumbers

Sea Cumcumbers inhabit the ocean floor. Most Sea Cumcumbers are found in deep oceans while a few species can be found in freshwaters as well. It is often seen partially buried on the ocean floor. It has a cylindrical shape which makes it look like a cucumber and hence its name.

It can be 0.75-6 feet in length. It feeds on algae and tiny sea organisms which it captures with its tube like feet that look like tentacles surrounding its mouth. When threatened, it releases sticky threads to misguide its predator. It can also contract its muscles forcibly as a defense mechanism.

INVERTEBRATES

INVERTEBRATES

227 Sea Spiders

Sea Spiders are called so because of their similar appearance to the land spider. It inhabits the world's oceans. It has a leg span of about 24 inches. It is rarely seen.

It can have anywhere from 4-6 pairs of legs. It has a small and slender body. It feeds on the body juices of Sea Anemone and Sponges. It has longer legs compared to the land spider. Its long legs enable it to move easily on the sea floor. Both male and female Sea Spiders have a pair of egg carrying legs.

228 Sea Stars

Sea Stars or Star Fish are found in all the world's oceans. Since it is not really a fish, it is now more often called a Sea Star. It is easily recognized by its five arms and hence its name. However, there have been species with more arms, even 20.

Its arms are located around a disc shaped body. It has a bony, calcified skin that protects it from predators. It has an amazing ability to generate its lost limbs, sometimes its entire body from a severed limb. Interestingly, it has no blood and no brain. It actually uses seawater to supply nutrients inside its body.

INVERTEBRATES

229 Squid

Squids mostly inhabit the cold waters of the world. It prefers to stay in deep waters and hence it is difficult to understand Squids.

It has a torpedo shaped body and eight arms with two long tentacles. It has the largest eyes in the animal kindom. Its large eyes help it to see in the ocean depths. Depending on the species Squids can be up to 33 feet in length. It is a fast moving and an intelligent invertebrate. Its torpedo shaped body helps it to propel through water. It swims by sucking water into its mantle cavity and by quickly removing it from its body though a nozzle like structure called siphon.

MAMMALS

230 Aardvark

Aardvark is native to Africa. Its name means 'earth pig' in Afrikaans. It is called so due to its resemblance to a pig and to its habit of digging. The Aardvark is 1.4-2.1 m long, including its 2 feet long tail. It has a long, narrow head, long ears and a blunt snout. Its teeth grow throughout its lifetime. It feeds on and searches for termites and ants in late evening and at night over a large home range. It has poor eyesight. It therefore swings its nose from side to side to pick up the scent of food. It can travel several miles in search of food. Once it has found a large termite mound or ant hill, it digs into it with its powerful front legs, keeping its ears upright to keep a lookout for predators. It can feed on about 50,000 insects in one night.

231 African Elephant

African Elephants are the largest land mammals. These mammals grow up to 8.2-13 feet tall at the shoulder. Both males and females have tusks. African Elephants have strong social bonds and live in herds under the leadership of a female elephant called a cow. Males elephants who are called bulls sometimes join the group. African Elephants use their enormous ears to radiate heat and to keep cool in the African heat. Interestingly, their ears are somewhat shaped like the African continent. They are fond of water and usually suck water through their trunks and spray it on themselves before coating their skin with mud and dust. These huge herbivores spend most of their time eating.

MAMMALS

232 African Wild Cat

African Wild Cats are found in the grasslands of Africa. They are also found in the Middle East. African Wild Cats are fierce cats. When the weather is warm they come out at night but when the weather is cold they are active during day.

African Wild Cat has powerful jaws and long, pointed canine teeth. It has sharp, retractable claws, a long tail and a striped coat that ranges from yellowish grey to light tan with a white throat and underbelly. These graceful cats are from 20-30 inches long. These carnivore cats hunt alone and are extremely good swimmers.

233 Agouti

Agouti is a rodent which is found in the rainforests of Mexico, Central America and northern South America. It is a fast running mammal. As a defence strategy against predators, they freeze.

Agouti coats have colours ranging from pale orange to brown to black. Agoutis have a very short tail, small, round ears and a large head. They are about 2.5 feet in length. These herbivores eat fruits, nuts, seeds, leaves and sometimes these rodents while eating disperse seeds on the forest floor.

MAMMALS

234 Alpaca

Alpaca are woolly mammals. These herding mammals are related to camels and Llamas. Alpacas are found in the Andes Mountains of western South America. These are smaller in size than the Llamas.

They have a small head, a long neck and large, pointed ears. Alpacas have long, thick, very soft hair on their bodies that vary in colour from white, grey to brown and black. Instead of hooves, Alpaca have thick pads at the bottom of their feet. Adult Alpacas are between 3-3.5 feet tall at the shoulders. These herbivores are bred for their soft wool. They cannot be made beasts of burden. They spit to show their fear, to give warning and sometimes to show their dominance.

235 Amazon River Dolphin

Pink Amazon River Dolphins are found not only in the Amazon River but also in the Orinoco Basin and the upper Madeira River. These dolphins are considered the most intelligent among the Dolphin species. They are generally 2.5 m in length. They feed on small freshwater fish and catfish. They have a bump on their back in place of a dorsal fin and a very flexible neck unlike other dolphins. The flexible neck allows them to look to the side and downwards.

These dolphins are also known with the names of 'boto', 'bufeo' and 'boutu'. The Amazon River Dolphins are curious by nature and are not afraid of coming near humans.

236 Antelope

Antelopes are mammals that are native to the grasslands of Africa and some parts of Asia. They have hollow horns on their heads which vary in size from being very long to short. Often, horns also vary in their shape and continue to grow throughout their lives. Females of the species also bear horns but they are smaller in size compared to those of the males. They have large eyes and ears which enable them to detect their predators.

Antelops are swift runners and graceful jumpers. These herbivores eat grass, shrubs, leaves and small shoots.

MAMMALS

237 Armadillo

Armadillo are native to the grasslands and forests of South America and also of Southern United States. Their name comes from a Spanish word which means 'little armoured one'. They are called so due to the bony plates that cover most of their body. They are the only mammals who wear such plates. The Armadillos vary in length from 5-59 inches.

Armadillos dig burrows where they sleep for many hours. They come out of their burrows to feed themselves on ants, termites and beetles. They rely on the strong sense of smell to catch their prey as they have poor eyesight.

Despite popular belief not all species of Armadillos can coil themselves into a ball when threatened by a predator.

238 Aye-Aye

Aye-Aye is a lemur which is native to the rainforests of Madagascar. It is related to Monkeys, Chimpanzees and Apes. It has large eyes and a long tail.

It comes out at night and likes being solitary. It spends a majority of its time on trees. They do not like coming down on the ground. It spends the day in a nest sleeping, curled up. It has pointed, clawed fingers and its middle finger is very long. Aye-Aye is an omnivore.

239 Baboon

Baboons are one of the largest monkeys in the world. It lives in the savannah and grasslands in Africa and the Arabian Peninsula. Baboons' bodies vary from 20-40 inches and the length of their tail varies. It lives in large groups called troops. Each troop is headed by a large and powerful male Baboon. These old world monkeys communicate with each other in a variety of voices.

It has a muscular body structure. The colour of their fur varies from grey to brown. Baboons have a somewhat doglike face structure. It is an omnivore. Leopards and Cheetahs are their biggest predators.

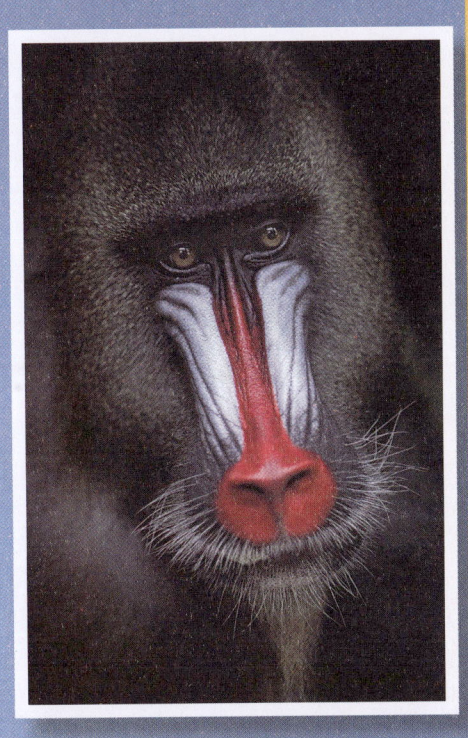

240 Bactrian Camel

Bactrian Camels are native to northern Asia. These two humped mammals are 7 feet tall. It has a coat of fur on its body. The amount of this fur thickens during the harsh winters and it falls in thickness as soon as the temperatures become warm.

Both male and female of the species have two humps. It can endure long periods of drought and food shortages. It is because it can use the stored fat in its hump during such times. it rarely sweats and thus conserves fluid in its hump. Interestingly, a thirsty Bactrian Camel can drink about 135 litres of water in merely 13 minutes!

241 Badger

Badgers are native to the grasslands, woodlands, and tropical forests of Asia, Europe and North America. Badgers are most active at night. It has a short, broad body and a bushy tail with a strip of a contrasting colour on its forehead.

It prefers to live in burrows. Its forelegs have powerful claws which it uses to dig burrows and also to find food.

It produces a strong smelling liquid called musk that it uses among other things to mark its territory. Badgers are omnivores. They eat rodents, frogs, snakes, worms, insects, fruits and roots.

242 Bat

Bats, the only flying mammals, are found all over the world except at the poles. Bats are most active at night. During day time they sleep hanging upside-down. With varied species, though they look similar in flight, their size varies and so does the colour of their fur. It is divided into two categories- Microchiroptera and Megachiroptera.

Microchiroptera includes those Bats that use echolocation (a high pitched sound emitted by the bat which returns to it after bouncing off objects) to find their way and food. On the other hand, Megachiroptera use their sense of smell to find their food.

Like other mammals, Bats too give birth to live young.

243 Bear

Bears are large, powerful mammals which are found on almost every continent.

There are 8 species of Bears in the world, some with a few sub species. These species include the Black Bears, Brown Bears, Polar Bears and Pandas among others.

During cold winter months, some Bears go into a dormant state called hibernation in which their heart rate becomes extremely low, their body temperature remains relatively high and they neither eat nor release bodily waste.

Most Bears are omnivores; Polar Bears are the only exception - they are carnivores. Bears despite their size can run extremely fast with a speed of up to 30 miles an hour.

244 Beaver

Beavers are one of the largest rodents. They are excellent swimmers though they walk on land with short steps swaying their body from side to side. They are native to the forests of North America but they are also found in parts of Europe and Asia.

It makes its house underwater using sticks, twigs and mud. The lodge, which is what its house is called, has underground entrances. A beaver makes a dam or dams downstream if the water in the pond or lake, where it wants to makes its lodge is shallow. Beavers store a large amount of food in their homes during spring and summer preparing for winters.

Beavers are herbivores, eating tree bark, leaves, roots, twigs, along with water plants. While swimming underwater transparent eyelids protect their eyes as they work to make their home.

MAMMALS

245 Bighorn Sheep

The Bighorn Sheep are found in the Rocky Mountains in North America. They are also found in some areas of Canada and Mexico. These mammals are 32-40 inches in length at the shoulder. Similar to goats, Bighorn Sheep are famous for their large, curled horns. The horns grow all their lives.

The male and female of the species live in separate herds. The Bighorn Sheep are also known for their head to head combats which take place to win over a female or to determine their rank. These battles can sometimes last for over a day!

Both male and female of the species have horns, though horns of the male are bigger. Made of keratin, the horns have growth rings which help to determine the sheep's age. As a herbivore, it spends its day grazing.

246 Binturong

Binturongs are mammals that are native to the dense forests of Southeast Asia. These carnivores grow up to a length of 60-96 cm. It has large, thick fur on its body. They also have a prehensile tail which almost acts like another leg while climbing and walking.

It lives on trees and is most active at night. It uses its keen sense of smell to find food. It is generally a solitary animal.

247 Bison

Bison is native to the Americas. It stands between 5-6.5 feet in length at the shoulders. Also called the American Buffalo, it is the heaviest land animal in North America. It lives in grasslands. Though the Bison is heavy, when the need arises it can run with speeds that reach up to 40 miles an hour.

The Bison has large horns on its head. Both male and female of the species have them. It has a hump on its back. The body of a Bison is covered with thick, coarse hair. The male and female of the species live in separate groups and come together to reproduce. Bison is a herbivore that feeds on grass, twigs and shrubs.

MAMMALS

248 Blue Whale

The Blue Whale is the largest mammal on earth. It inhabits almost all the seas of the world. It can grow up to 82-105 feet in length. They weigh up to 150 tons. These magnificent mammals rule the seas. It has a broad, flat head which is attached to a long body. It travels through the sea at five miles an hour.

Interestingly, even baby Blue Whales weigh more than an elephant and are 25 feet in length when they are born. They grow up fast. It gains almost 200 pounds each day in the first year after it's born.

Blue Whales feed on an enormous diet of krills. They are the loudest animals on the earth and sometimes they can hear each other over a distance of 1000 miles. Its heart is as large as a small car!

MAMMALS

249 Bobcat

Bobcats are native to North America. These fast, solitary and fierce cats can live in almost any habitat. It is most active at night and is rarely spotted.

Often called Wildcats, it has long legs, big paws and is bigger than the average cat. It is named so because of its tail which appears as if it is cut or 'bobbed'. It is an excellent climber and can swim efficiently. It is a carnivore and eats small animals like rabbits, mice and squirrels. It kills its prey slyly. It pounces on its prey by leaping. Its leap can cover up to 10 feet.

250 Bongo

Bongo is a species of antelopes that are found in almost all parts of Africa. It is among the largest antelopes. It has a brown coat, from light to dark, with white or cream spots or stripes. The stripes and the colour of its fur helps it to remain camouflaged in shade.

Its sense of hearing is strong and its hearing skills make it aware of the presence of predators. It has a long prehensile tongue which helps it to reach and grab leaves which are high up the tree. Bongos have horns on their heads. It is most active at night, is a fast runner and jumps very well. Both male and female of the species have horns that grow all through their lives.

251 Capybara

Capybara, the world's biggest rodent, is native to South America. It is found in swamps, ponds and lakes. It grows to about 1.4 m in length.

Capybaras live in a group of about 20 animals. Generally, the group is headed by a dominant male; others in the group include females and the young ones. The body of the Capybara is covered with thin brown fur. Since the mammal spends a lot of time in water, its fur dries off quickly. The webbed skin between its toes helps it to swim in water.

It is a herbivore and it feeds on water plants, grass and fruits.

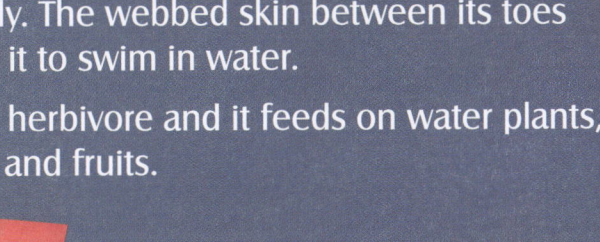

252 Caribou

Caribou is native to the northern North America, Europe, Asia and it is even found in Greenland. Caribou is commonly known as the reindeer. It is about 4-5 feet at the shoulder. Both male and female of the species have wide antlers.

Each year as summer approaches, huge herds of Caribou migrate towards the north. It is one of the largest animal migrations in the world. They can travel up to 600 miles during the migration. Some even cover greater distances.

During summer they spend time eating grasses. They have large hooves that help it to support itself on the snow and also to find food.

MAMMALS

253 Cheetah

Cheetah, one among the big cats, is the fastest land animal in the world. It can go from 0 to 60 miles per hour in merely 3 seconds. Extremely flexible, Cheetahs can turn suddenly and quickly even at great speeds. It is native to the eastern and southwestern Africa.

It has an exceptional eyesight. They look about the grasslands for even a slightest movement to locate their prey. It is about 3.5-4.5 feet in length. It has a spotted coat which helps it to remain hidden while stalking its prey in the grasslands. Once it has caught its prey, it must hide it or eat it quickly before hyenas or lions come along to snatch the Cheetah's prey.

254 Chimpanzee

Chimpanzees are the closest relatives of human beings. It is a very intelligent ape that is native to the rainforests and grasslands of western and central Africa. At about 4-5.5 feet tall, these great apes live in groups. Sometimes these groups can have up to 100 individuals.

Chimpanzees' bodies are covered with hair, except their face, toes, fingers and the bottom. Their hands are longer than their legs. Though they walk on four legs, these great apes can also walk straight on two legs. They spend most of their time on trees, and often swing from tree to tree efficiently. They are plant-eaters but they can also eat insects, eggs and meat.

In a recent discovery, it was learnt that Chimpanzees can use tools. They use sticks to drive out insects from their holes, they use rocks to smash open nuts and employ leaves as sponges to soak up water to drink.

255 Chinchilla

Chinchilla is a rodent that is native to South America. It lives in the rock crevices and burrows in the Andes Mountains.

It grows up to 23 to 38 cms in length. It has a blue grey or brown fur which is the softest and the densest fur in the world. It is a herbivore and eats grass, seeds, fruits and herbs. Like all rodents, their two front teeth grow throughout their lives and therefore they must gnaw at something to wear them down.

Females of the species are larger than the males. It has an acute sight and keen hearing which often helps it to escape its predators.

256 Chipmunk

Chipmunks are native to North America, Europe and Asia. They are often seen in a variety of habitats. At about 10-18 inches, Chipmunks are the smallest members of the squirrel family. They have a long bushy tail. Their fur varies in colour from grey to red and brown. They have light or dark lines on their back, tail and face.

Many Chipmunks dig burrows to live in. These burrows can be extensive but some species even live in nests, bushes or logs of wood. They feed on seeds, nuts, grains and fruits and sometimes insects. They stuff their food in cheek pouches and bring it to their burrows or nests for storage.

Like some animals, Chipmunks hibernate. But instead of using the fat stored in their bodies, they often get up from their hibernation and slowly eat the food they had stored.

MAMMALS

MAMMALS

257 Coati

Coati, also called Coatimundi, is a native of south western United States and also of South America. It belongs to the racoon family. They are usually seen in the woodlands. It has a large and mostly flexible snout and a long banded tail. It more than often keeps its ringed tail erect as it walks.

This small mammal measures 73–136 cms in length, which also includes its tail. It has brown to red fur. The female and the young live in small groups called bands. The males live a solitary life. It can climb trees efficiently.

It is omnivorous. It can eat seeds, fruits, nuts, bird eggs, insects and small rodents.

258 Coyote

Coyote is found all over North America. It is closely related to the wolves. It has adapted itself marvellously and can live in all types of habitats. It grows to about 81-94 cms in length and its tail is 41 cms long.

This clever animal can have a brown, grey or cream coat. This fast running carnivore has a keen sense of smell, excellent eyesight and sharp hearing. Coyote is also a good swimmer. It can reach speeds of up to 40 miles while running. The colour of their coat hides them when they hunt their prey. It can eat almost anything.

Coyotes live in family groups and both the parents' guards their young and their territory fiercely.

259 Dall's Porpoise

Dall's Porpoise is found in the North Pacific Ocean and the seas adjoining it. It is called so after an American Naturalist, W. H. Dall, who had identified and classified them.

It measures between 1.8-2 metres in length. It has an extremely stocky and powerful body. It is a fast swimmer and can cruise the seas with a speed of 34 mph. They often swim in a zigzag pattern taking sharp turns. When swimming speedily, it makes a 'rooster tail' splash. It is called so because the splashing water looks like a rooster's tail.

It is normally seen in groups of 12 individuals but much larger groups are also seen. They are distinguished from other porpoises by their distinctive white patch on a black body.

260 Deer

Deer has 44 species which are found almost on every continent. It is found in habitats ranging from forests, grasslands, fields and the tundra. The Moose is the largest among the deer family while the Andean Pudu is the smallest.

Deer has a four-chambered stomach. It has hoofed feet, long legs and a red to brown colour coat to hide itself from the predators. It has an elongated snout and a short tail. Male deer grow antlers which they shed each spring only to be replaced by new ones.

Deer are plant eaters. They eat leaves, grass shoots, twigs and small shrubs. They spent most of their time grazing. They can run fast and often take long leaps.

MAMMALS

MAMMALS

261 Duck-billed Platypus

Duck-billed Platypus is native to eastern Australia. This mammal is quite unique for it lays eggs instead of giving birth to young ones.

Its body is about 47 cms in length. It has a grey to brown thick fur on its body which keeps it warm even when it is in water. It has a broad, flat tail which looks like that of a beaver. Its body and head too is flattened.

Its feet are webbed and help it to swim excellently. The most interesting thing about Platypus is its snout which resembles a duck and hence its name. Its snout is covered with a smooth, leathery skin. To make it look stranger, male platypus are venomous. The male platypus has a spur on its hind ankles that is connected to a venom sac in each leg. Though not fatal, the venom is very painful.

262 Dugong

Dugong is found in the warm waters that surround Indonesia and Australia. They can also be found in the Indian Ocean, the Red Sea and in the waters surrounding east Africa. This large vegetarian is about 8-10 feet in length.

It grazes the sea grass day and night. It must come to the water surface after every six minutes to breathe. Sometimes, they stand on their tail, bring their faces above water and breathe.

It is seen either solitary or in a pair. They are also sometimes seen gathered in the hundreds. It is thought that the legends of mermaids may have originated from them. Sailors may perhaps when seeing them from a distance mistook them to be mermaids.

263 Echidna

Echinda is native to Australia and New Guinea. It is found in coastal forests, meadows and deserts. It has sharp spines all over its short, stocky body. It has a long snout which helps it to detect and break termite mounds which are its favourite food. Echinda can grow to be 35 to 53 cms long.

It has a sticky tongue that is ideal for catching insects and termites. Its fore feet have five claws which are used for digging. When it is threatened, it curls into a ball exposing its sharp spikes. With a keen sense of smell, an Echidna uses its long, hairless snout to find food and also to detect danger.

264 Ferret

Ferrets are found in the prairies and grasslands of North America. They are most active at night. They are 38-50 cms in length. Its long, slender body allows it to easily enter the burrows of the prairie dogs to eat the food there and then uses the same burrows to seek shelter.

Sometimes they also eat mice, squirrels and other rodents as well. It sleeps for about 21 hours and hunts at night. Ferrets are solitary animals and they live alone.

MAMMALS

265 Flying Squirrel

Flying Squirrels are found on almost every continent. They are found in woodlands and grasslands. Flying Squirrels do not actually fly. It rather glides from tree to tree. It has a flap of loose skin that connects its front and hind legs. When the squirrel wants to go somewhere quickly, it spreads its arms and legs, the membrane spreads like a parachute and the squirrel seems to be flying.

It can glide for up to 90 metres. When it lands on a tree, it grips the branch of the tree with its four feet. It is about 20-30 cms in length. It has brown to grey fur, large eyes and clawed feet. It lives in nests. It mostly feeds on seeds, nuts, leaves, bark, flowers and roots. It is most active at night.

266 Fossa

Fossa is native to the island of Madagascar. It is the largest predator on the island. Related to the Mongoose family and its largest member in terms of size, Foosa is very agile. It is a fast runner and is very good at climbing trees.

It has a slender body with large eyes, sharp teeth and retractable claws. Its muzzle looks like that of a dog. It has a long tail which helps it to balance and also assists while it jumps. It is about 60-76 cms long with a tail that is 71 cms long. It is a carnivore and it hunts lemurs, rodents, snakes, insects, chickens and small pigs.

267 Fox

Fox is naturally a widely distributed mammal. It is found in Asia, Europe, Africa, Australia and the America's. It can live in a variety of habitats. It is a symbol of animal cleverness and intelligence.

It is about 90-105 cms long with a 40 cms long tail. Its long bushy tail helps the animal to balance itself and change direction quickly. It is also used as a warm cover in cold environments. This carnivore has a thick, reddish brown fur coat. It hunts rodents, rabbit, bird, fish but it can also eat fruits and vegetables.

268 Gazelle

Gazelles are antelopes that are found both in Asia and Africa. These mammals live in herds, which can contain from a few to a hundred Gazelles, on dry grasslands and are also seen near deserts. It extracts water from the plants it eats. Thus, it does not have to drink water often.

It stands at about 51-109 cms at the shoulder. It has long, ringed horns that add to its beauty. The horns can be straight or curved. It is a swift runner which can jump very well. It also practices pronking, which is bouncing with all four legs held in a stiff position. In pronking, all of its four hoofed feet leave the ground and land at the same time. Gazelles are herbivores. It eats grasses, shoots and leaves.

MAMMALS

MAMMALS

269 Giant Otter

Giant Otters are native to the rainforests and rivers of South America. At about 6 feet long, it is the largest otter in the world. It has a brown fur coat which is thick and velvety to touch. It has a powerful tail, water repellent fur and webbed feet. A white mark on an individual's neck helps to distinguish between individuals. It closes its ears and nose when underwater.

Giant Otter's main food is fish. It lives in groups and often they hunt in groups. It makes it burrows on river banks or under fallen logs.

270 Gibbon

Gibbons are native to the dense rainforests of Southeast Asia. These small primates spend almost all their time on trees, swinging. It grows up to 44-64 cms long. It has long, slender arms which are longer than its legs. Its body is covered with thick fur except its face, palms, fingers and bottom of the feet.

Like humans, it has four fingers in its hands and a thumb and has five toes. Gibbons are omnivores as they feed on fruits, leaves, insects, spiders, small birds, seeds and flowers.

These acrobatic animals travel through the forest in their unique style of swinging called brachiating. This style of swinging allows them to travel at 35 mph through the forests. This method also allows it to grab its favourite fruits.

It stays in groups. It rarely walks on ground and when it does, it walks on its two feet, raising its arms over the head to maintain its balance. Even on trees, it often walks in a similar manner. They are often studied to find out how humans first started walking.

271 Giraffe

Giraffe are native to the savannahs of Africa. It is the tallest animal with a long neck and long legs. A Giraffe can be as tall as 14-19 feet.

A Giraffe is also unique because of its spots which are like fingerprints. No two Giraffes have the same pattern of spots. A long neck allows the Giraffe to reach the leaves from the top of trees which other animals cannot do. Its main food is the acacia plant. With their height, a Giraffe can also keep a look out for predators.

Giraffes do not drink water often. It is because it eats the moisture filled acacia leaves. When they do drink water, they can drink as much as 10 gallons or 38 litres a day.

It can run as fast as 35 mph. It continues to travel looking for food in small groups.

272 Gnu

Gnu also known as Wildebeest is native to the African continent. It is primarily found in the grasslands of south-eastern Africa. Its fur coat varies from grey to brown. It can grow up to 5 feet tall. It has a large head, pointed beard and sharp, curved horn.

It is seen in large herds and It spends its time grazing. They are known for their yearly northward migration, mostly in May and June, in search for green pastures. This migration includes more than a million Gnu along with Zebras and Gazelles.

Newborn calves can stand merely 3 to 5 minutes after they are born. It is soon after that they can run with the herd.

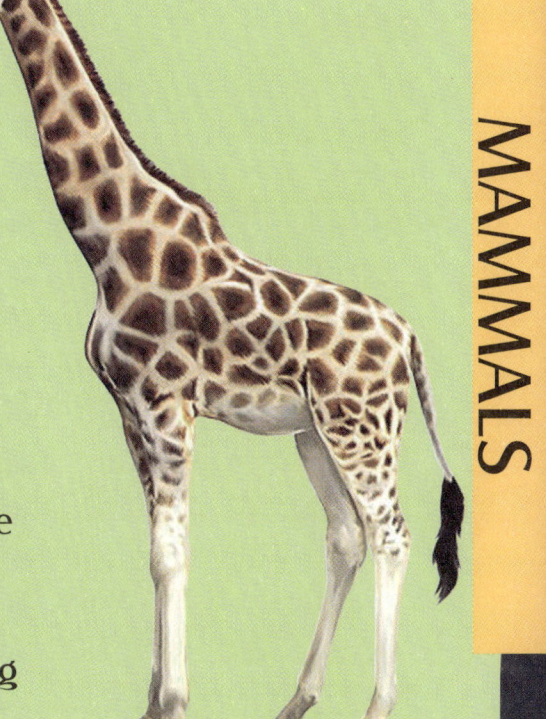

MAMMALS

MAMMALS

273 Golden Lion Tamarin

Golden Lion Tamarin are native to the tropical rainforests of Brazil. They are called so because of their golden manes. It is 19-22 cms in length with a tail that is 26-34 m long. These rare primates live in small social groups. It lives in trees and is most active during daytime.

It is covered with long, silky, gold-coloured fur though its face, hands and feet are bare. It feeds on insects, fruits, snakes, lizards and birds. They sleep in tree hollows at night.

Male and female together bring up their offspring.

274 Gorilla

Gorillas are found on the African continent. These large primates which are 4-6 feet in length are shy by nature. They can however turn aggressive when provoked. Its body is covered with black hair except the face, fingers and feet. It has a large head and broad, powerful chest. Its arms are longer than its legs.

Gorillas live in small groups comprising of a large, strong male, along with other males and females and their offspring. It can stand upright, throw things and pound its broad chest while making threatening calls and shouts to the intruder. They feed on leaves and fruits.

275 Hares

Hares are small mammals that are found in nearly all parts of the world. It can live in a variety of habitats ranging from forests to grasslands and even in the Arctic. Hares have long ears with strong hind legs. It is related to the rabbits but it is larger of the two.

Hares can vary in sizes from 36-71 cms long with tails as long as 5 to 10 cms. Even the colour of their fur varies from white, brown to grey and red. They have two front teeth that grow all through their lives just like rodents. It eats leaves, grass and herbs. Newborn Hares have fur on their bodies and their eyes are open unlike rabbits. It is just a matter of minutes before the newborn Hares start hopping with their parents.

MAMMALS

276 Hedgehog

Hedgehogs are found in Asia, Africa and Europe. It can live in a vast variety of habitats ranging from grasslands, forests, deserts and plains. This small mammal is 13 to 30 cms in length and has a small tail.

It is called so because of its hunting technique. While looking for food, as it picks its way through the hedges, he makes sounds which resemble a pig's grunt. Its coat of fur ends in sharp, spiky spines. When threatened, it curls itself into a ball and it becomes impossible to attack it.

In colder climates, Hedgehogs hibernate while in deserts they sleep during the day in a process called aestivate.

MAMMALS

277 Hippopotamus

Hippopotamus are native to Africa. In Greek, its name means 'river horse'. It is considered the largest mammal after the African Elephant and the White Rhinoceros. It is usually seen half submerged in rivers, ponds and swamps. It does so to beat the heat in Africa.

This large mammal has small ears, small eyes with half a metre wide mouth. It is 9 to 14 feet long with short, thick legs. Its thick skin is nearly hairless. It can stay submerged under water for about 5-6 minutes.

These large herbivores come out to graze at night. Though they have a massive size, they can run as fast as humans.

278 Horses

Horses are among the fastest running mammals. It is found on all the continents. Many of its species have been domesticated while others stay in the wild in grasslands and plains. These large mammals were first domesticated about 4000 years ago.

Horses are herbivores and they graze grasses. It has hoofed feet. Its hooves continue to grow all its life. It has large eyes and ears to see and detect predators and a long narrow mane on its neck. Did you know that Horses sleep while standing!

279 Hyena

Hyena is found in Africa, in some parts of the Middle East and in Asia. Its habitat includes savannah and dry plains. These scavengers are skilled hunters with sharp eyesight and excellent hearing.

It lives in groups called clans. These groups are led by a female. They hunt in groups. Its prey includes Gnu and Antelope, Zebra and Gazelle though they are also seen hunting smaller animals. It has sharp teeth and powerful jaws that allow it to even eat the bones of its prey.

It makes a giggling sound to communicate. Hence, it is also called laughing hyena. Though they look like dogs but they are related to cats.

280 Jaguar

Jaguars are native to South and Central America. They live in grasslands, rainforests and near swamps. It is one of the big cats which are now threatened. Jaguars live alone and are territorial. They are excellent swimmers and do not shy away from eating fish and turtles. They also hunt Deer, Capybara and Tapirs.

It grows up to 5-6 feet long. Its brown or orange coat is covered with black spots. These graceful hunters can even climb trees. From there, they can leap on their prey and kill it at once. Though seen during day, they go hunting at night.

MAMMALS

281 Karakul

Karakul is a breed of sheep that is found in central and west Asia. These sheep are domesticated for their smooth, soft fur. The colour of their coats varies from black to brown and shades of grey.

Karakul may be the oldest domesticated breed of sheep. Its strong fibres are used to make carpets. Karakuls have a wide, fat tail where they store fat. The lambs are born with usually black fleece which becomes of lighter shade as they grow. Male Karakul sheep have curved horns that grow all their lives. These sheep are also known to survive for long in harsh climates.

282 Killer Whale (Orca)

Orca or Killer Whales are found in cold, coastal waters across the globe. These largest members of the dolphin family are distinguished by the white patches on its underside and near its eyes. It can grow 23-32 feet long. They have large dorsal fins. As one of the world largest predators, it eats Seals, Sea Lions, Squids, sea birds and sometimes the Blue Whale. It hunts in groups. It makes distinctive sounds that can be heard by its group members from a distance.

283 Leopard Seal

Leopard Seal is native to the Antarctic and its surrounding waters. It is called so because of the spots on its skin just like that of the big cat. It is among the largest seals in the world. It grows to about 10-12 feet.

It is a fierce predator and hunts on other warm blooded animals like smaller seals. It powerful jaws and sharp teeth allow it to easily kill fish, Penguins and Squids. It does not have ears and its body is covered with thick layer of fat called blubber.

MAMMALS

284 Leopard

Leopards are found in Africa, Central Asia, India and China. They live in a variety of habitats ranging from grasslands, plains, deserts and forests. It measures from 4-6 feet and has a 3-4.5 feet long tail. Due to its spotted coat, Leopards are able to easily blend in with the tall grasses.

It is a fast runner, skilled swimmer and excellent tree climber. Often after it has caught and killed its prey, it takes the prey to a tree to eat it. It does so also to keep its kill away from hyenas.

MAMMALS

285 Lion

Lions, among the largest cats, are found in Africa and in India. These fierce cats roam in grasslands and the savannas. It grows up to 6 feet in length.

Lions live in a group of about 15 or more lions called a Pride. In a pride, lionesses do the hunting while the male lions defend their territory. A pride can have a territory of about 100 square miles. Male lions have manes which makes them look fierce. A Lion's roar can be heard as far as 5 miles away. The darker the mane of a Lion, the older he is.

286 Llamas

Llamas are found in the Andes Mountains in South America. It is related to the camel. It has been domesticated in the Andes Mountains for thousand of years. It is 119 cms at the shoulder.

Llamas are pack animals. It can pick up loads of between 23–34 kgs. With such load it can travel to a distance of 20 miles. It is also raised for its wool and meat. Even its droppings are burned as fuel. It does not have hooves. It has a two-toed foot with toenails on top and pads at the bottom. These herbivores eat grass, herbs and small plants.

287 Lynx

Lynx are fierce cats that are found in North America, Europe and Asia. Their habitat includes forests. It is a cunning animal and it hunts at night. It lives a solitary life.

It has a beautiful, thick coat to warm itself in the harsh winters. With its large paws it moves quietly. It has sharp and pointed teeth and strong jaws. It has acute hearing which allow it to detect its prey from a distance.

Lynx has tufts of hair on its ears. It is 2-3 feet long with a 4-8 inches long tail. It is a carnivore which hunts Rabbits, Fox, Weasels and small deer.

288 Mandrill

Mandrills are the world's largest monkeys. These old world monkeys are found in the rainforests of equatorial Africa. It has blue and red facial markings which make it stand apart. It spends its time on trees and when on ground, it walks on all fours.

Mandrill has very long canine teeth. It is 3 feet long. Mandrill has hair all over his body except his face and bottoms. Even its bottom is brightly coloured. It lives in groups called troops. A troop is headed by a male. It is a herbivore which eats leaves, fruits. But it can also eat small insects and snakes.

MAMMALS

MAMMALS

289 Maui's Dolphin

Maui's Dolphin is the smallest dolphin in the world. It is found only on the north-west coast of the north island of New Zealand. It is mostly found close to the shore. It has a short snout and a rounded dorsal fin. It is so small with only 1.7 metres long that it can be easily kept in a bathtub. It spends most of its time feeding.

As its global population is extremely less, with only 55 individuals remaining in the world, it is critically endangered. It's slow breeding rate is also responsible for their endangered status.

290 Meerkat

Meerkat is a small mammal that lives in the harsh climate of Southern Africa. It is a member of the Mongoose family and is very social. Meerkats are known for their upright posture, where they stand on their hind legs and gaze at their surroundings.

It lives in groups. Often many families live together. They also like to work together. While some Meerkats work, play or eat, the others stand on their hind legs to watch out for predators like eagle, hawks and jackals.

It lives in burrows which are extensively made. It contains several rooms and long tunnels.

291 Mink

Mink is a member of the weasel family. It is native to North America, Europe and West Asia. It lives near rivers, streams, marshes and swamps. Mink are semi-aquatic animals. It is about 30-50 cms in length.

It has a pointed snout, short legs, small ears and a long, thick neck. It has a coat that varies from brown to black. It is hunted for its fur and is also bred in captivity.

It looks for its food in the waters as well as near it. It feeds on frogs, hares, salamander and crayfish.

292 Mole

Moles are found in North America, Asia, Europe and some parts of Africa. It can live in a variety of habitats ranging from swamps, river banks, deserts, forests and even fields. It lives in burrows. Moles have very small eyes but they are blind.

It is therefore that moles have heightened sense of touch. It has sensory bumps on the snout, sensory whiskers on the face, and sensory hairs on its feet and tail as well. It is about 2-9 inches in length. It has clawed feet which it uses to dig burrows. It also has a long, powerful tail.

It is an insectivore and it eats as many insects as its body weight each day.

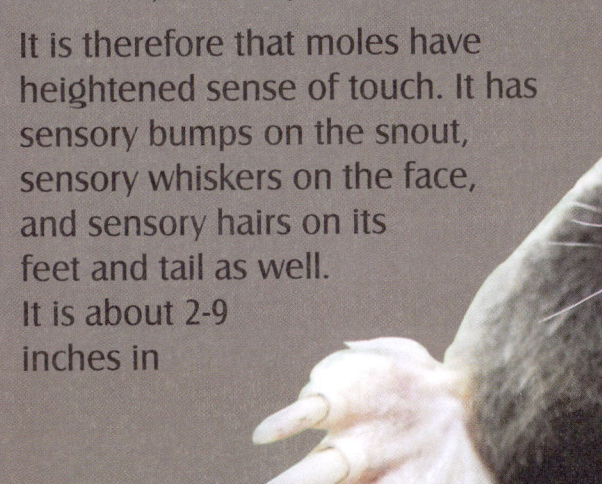

MAMMALS

MAMMALS

293 Mongoose

Mongoose is mostly native to most of Africa but they are also found in southern Asia. It can live in various habitats ranging from forest, marshes and grasslands. It is a sleek mammal having a long body with short legs, long tail and a tapered mouth. It can be upto 2 feet long depending on the species. Its coat can be from brown to grey.

It has sharp claws which it uses to dig burrows and to catch its prey. It eats insects, worms, frog, snakes and birds. Interestingly, some species of Mongoose are known to attack venomous snakes like the King Cobra.

294 Moose

Moose is the largest among the deer family. It is native to North America, Europe and Russia. They are also known for their antlers. The antlers of a Moose can grow up to be 6 feet long from end to end.

Moose can be 5-6.5 feet at the shoulder. It has large hooves that act as snowshoes in snow. Its body is covered with brown fur and from its throat hangs a flap of skin called bell. It is a solitary animal that grazes grasses, moss, lichen, pond weeds and shrubs. It is a good swimmer and can swim for miles. When on land, it can run with a speed of 35 miles an hour.

295 Narwhal

Narwhals are found in the Arctic Sea. It is also called 'the unicorn of the ocean' because of a large tusk on its face. It is not easily seen and it has a rather mysterious nature.

A Narwhal can be from 13-20 feet long. Its tusk is actually a tooth that had grown in a spiral shape out of the male's upper lip. It can be as long as 7-10 feet. The females too grow a tusk but it is not as long as that of the male.

It is extremely rare that the Narwhals go away from the icy waters of the Arctic Sea. They are usually seen in large groups called pods.

296 Okapi

Okapi are found in the Congo River Basin in Central Africa. It was first discovered in 1901 by a British explorer. It is related to the giraffe though it is not as tall. It is a solitary animal which is most active at night.

Okapi has a brown coat and its face sides are white. It has horizontal white stripes on its forelegs and bottom. It can grow to about 5 feet in length. It has a long tongue. It uses its tongue to strip leaves from the branches.

Male Okapi have small horns. Its horns are covered with fur except at the tips. Females do not have horns though they have knobby bumps where the horns should be.

MAMMALS

MAMMALS

297 Orangutan

Orangutan's are native only to the rainforests of Sumatra and Borneo. These primates' name means, 'person of the forest' in Malay. Orangutans are extremely intelligent and are close relatives of humans.

Orangutans can be 4-5 feet in length. They have very long arms. When it stands up, its arms touch the ground. As these primates spend most of their time on trees, their long arms are well suited for their environment. Its body is covered with orange-red long hair. An Orangutan makes Its bed using large leaves and sleeps on the tree.

This omnivore swings from tree to tree using Its long arms to find food or to play.

298 Oryx

Oryx is found in Africa and the Arabian Peninsula. It lives in the dry plains and deserts of the region. It is a fast running mammal and is powerfully built.

Oryx has a striking colour combination. It has a brownish coat with contrasting black and white stripes. It also has long, sharp, ringed horns. It usually lives in large herds that can be about 60-70 Oryx strong. It is a herbivore that eats grasses, shrubs and roots. It can go without water in scarcity but when water is available, it drinks freely.

299 Panda

Giant Pandas are native to the mountainous regions of China. It is a black-and-white bear that loves to eat bamboo trees. A Giant Panda can eat up to 12.5 kgs of bamboo to satisfy its hunger in a day.

It is a large mammal with a big head, a heavy body, rounded ears and a short tail. It is white mammal with black patches around its eyes, ears, shoulders, chest, legs and feet. They are excellent tree climbers and can swim very efficiently. It lives a solitary live and has a heightened sense of smell.

300 Pangolin

Pangolins are found in tropical Asia and Africa. Its body is covered in razor-sharp scales. When this small mammal is threatened it curls itself into a ball exposing its sharp scales.

Pangolins are 1-3 feet long. It has a short, conical head, a toothless muzzle and a long tongue. Its short legs have sharp claws. It eats termites, ants and other insects. It has a strong sense of smell and it locates its prey using its sense of smell.

It is nocturnal. Pangolins, depending on the species, can live in hollow trees or in tunnels. It is also a good swimmer.

MAMMALS

301 Panther

Panther is native to Asia, Africa and the Americas. Its habitat ranges from forests, grasslands and even to deserts. It is a black coloured feline belonging to the big cat family. It is a strong climber and an excellent swimmer.

Unlike other cats like Leopard and Jaguar, it has no spots on its fur. Its body is covered in a coat of black fur. It has a keen eyesight and good hearing. It has powerful jaws, pointed canine teeth and sharp, retractable claws. It can be as long as 6 feet with a 2-3 feet long tail. It is a carnivore and a solitary hunter.

302 Polar Bear

Polar Bears are found in the Arctic ice sheets. These powerful mammals swim the Arctic Sea wonderfully. It has a thick layer of body fat and its insulated fur is water repellent. It is about 8 feet in length at the shoulder.

Did you know that Polar Bears have black skin under its stark white fur!

It has a small head with a powerful jaw. Its front paws are slightly webbed and help it in swimming. It has a strong sense of smell. It can smell its favourite food seal from some 32 kms away. They stalk areas where ice breaks in search of food.

303 Porcupine

Porcupines are found in North America, Asia, Africa and Europe. They inhabit grasslands, forests and even deserts. The North American Porcupine is the largest porcupine.

Its body is covered with hair but they are usually mixed with sharp quills. The quills usually lie flat. But when the Porcupine is threatened, the quills stand upright challenging the predator to dare attack it. When the quills get stuck into the predator's body, it is difficult to remove them. It is also a good climber and likes to spend its time on trees. This herbivore eats leaves, bark, fruits and buds.

MAMMALS

304 Puma

Puma is found in North America. Its habitat includes deserts and fields but it can also be found near swamps and forests. It is also called Mountain Lion or Cougar. It has tan or brown colour coat. One among the large cats, it is a ruthless hunter.

It stalks its prey and waits patiently to ambush its prey. It usually hunts at night.

Puma is a solitary animal and usually avoids human habitation. But it sometimes hunts livestock.

MAMMALS

305 Raccoon

Raccoons are small mammals that are native to North America. They live in a variety of habitats including forest, prairies, marshes and even cities. It is a highly adaptable mammal. It is most active at night.

Raccoons are easily recognized by the distinctive black patches around their eyes. The patches seem like a mask. It has lightening-quick paws that allow it to eat a variety of animals. It feeds on crayfish, mice, frogs, insects, fruits, plants and it can even be found digging in the garbage bin. Raccoons like their adaptable nature live in hollow tree trunks, fallen logs and can even be found in attics.

306 Red Kangaroo

Red Kangaroo is found on the Australian continent. It does not walk but hopes everywhere on its powerful hind legs. It can grow up to be 5 feet tall with a tail that measures 35-43 inches.

While hopping, a Red Kangaroo can reach great speeds. Female Red Kangaroos are smaller and faster than the males. Females also have a blue-hued coat and therefore, it is also called 'blue fliers'.

While it hops, it can cover a distance of 25 feet with each hop. During a fight, kangaroos lean back on their strong tail and 'box' each other using its powerful hind legs.

307 Reindeer

Reindeers are found in the Arctic Tundra, Canada, Scandinavia, Northern China and Russia. In North America, it is called 'caribou'. It can be 4 feet in length at the shoulder.

Reindeers have been domesticated in various places for many years. As it lives in a cold environment, it has adapted likewise to its surroundings. It has deeply cloven hoofs that allow it to run and walk on the snow easily. It is also known for its long distance migrations towards the north during the summer months.

MAMMALS

308 Rhinoceros

Rhinoceros is found in only a few places in the world. It lives in grasslands. It is known for its one or two horns. Its horn is made of keratin, the same substance that is found in our hair. Rhinoceros can be up to 12 feet long.

It is a large mammal with thick skin. Its skin acts like an armour. It has a keen sense of hearing and smell. They are more or less hairless. Despite its massive bulk, a Rhinoceros can run fast. This massive herbivore eats grass, fruits and leaves. It is a solitary animal.

MAMMALS

309 Ring-tailed Lemur

Ring-tailed Lemurs are native to the rainforests on the island of Madagascar. They are also seen in scrubs and rocky areas. It is distinguished by its striking long, black and white tail. It is a noisy mammal.

It uses its hands and feet to walk on the trees but it does not use its tail. Unlike the other primates, it spends a lot of time on the ground. It eats fruit, leaves, flowers and insects. It has a powerful scent gland. It is used to communicate with other lemurs and also sometimes as a weapon. It lives in groups called troops. The troops are headed by a female.

310 Ross Seal

Ross Seals are found in the Arctic waters. It is also known as big-eyed seal because it has big eyes. It is rarely seen. Sometimes, it is seen resting on the ice. It is named after the British explorer James Clark Ross, who found the first specimen. It is 5-9 feet long. It has a slender body with a thick neck. Its coat is dark grey or brown. It can dive several hundred metres to catch its prey. It feeds on fish, squid and krill. It is hunted by Killer Whales and Leopard Seals.

311 Siamang

Siamang is native to the rainforests of Malaysia and Indonesia. It is the largest among all the Gibbon species. It has long arms and spends most of its time on trees. It is covered in thick, dense, black hair all over its body except its face, palms, fingers and bottom of its feet.

It travels through the forest using a technique called brachiation. In it, Siamangs swing from branch to branch using its long arms. On high branches, it walks like a tightrope walker with outstretched arms to keep its balance. Both male and female Siamangs have voice sac which are inflated to make the calls louder.

312 Slender Loris

Slender Loris is native to the deciduous forests of India and Sri Lanka. It is a small mammal that lives on trees. It is about 25 cm in length. It has long, thin arms. Among its distinguishing feature are a set of large eyes. They move on the trees slowly using their unusual toes. On each of his toes it has an opposing big toe which gives it a four-way grip on the branch. It hunts in pairs and when threatened it runs to the safety of the thickest part of the trees very fast. It feeds on insects.

MAMMALS

MAMMALS

313 Sloth

Sloth is native to the rainforests of central and South America. It is the slowest mammal on the earth! It spends all its life living on the trees. It is so inactive that green algae grows on its fur.

It is 58 cms long and has long, prominent claws. It spends a majority of its time hanging upside-down from the trees. This herbivore eats leaves, tender young shoots and fruit. It nearly sleeps between 15-20 hours. And though this mammal cannot walk due its weak limbs, it swims very well.

314 Snow Leopard

Snow Leopards are native to the mountains of Central Asia. It is a grey coloured cat with thick insulated fur to keep out the cold. It also has wide fur covered feet to help it walk easily on the snow.

It is about 4-5 feet long with a long tail. Snow Leopards can leap various feet in one bound. It has powerful legs and it uses its tail for balance while it leaps. It feeds on large prey but it can also eat small mammals like hares. It is hunted for its thick fur and for its body parts which are used in traditional Chinese medicines.

315 Steller's Sea Cow

Steller's Sea Cow was a large aquatic mammal. It was about 26-30 feet long. It was first discovered in 1741 by German biologist Georg Steller in the Bering Sea. It became extinct 25-30 years after it was first discovered.

This large herbivore had a small head, a broad tail fluke. It had a brown coat with either white stripes or spots. It had small flippers in the front part of its body that helped it to move in water. It was much larger than present day Dugong and Manatees. It floated near the sea surface making it an easy target for the hunters.

316 Tapir

Tapirs are primarily found in the grasslands and forests of central and South America. The largest Tapir is found in Southeast Asia. Tapirs are recognized by its short trunk which is actually its extended nose and falls on its upper lip.

Tapir uses its long trunk to grab branches and pluck leaves from them. It follows known trails which are usually near water. Tapirs like to spent time near water and are often found submerged in water. It is about 29-42 inches at the shoulder. They are good swimmers and also like to wallow in mud.

MAMMALS

317 Tarsier

Tarsier is a small primate that is native to some islands of Southeast Asia, mainly Malaysia. This primate spends most of its time on trees. It has many distinctive features including large eyes and a long tail. The long fingers of the Tarsier have pads at its ends and its long hind feet help it to leap from tree to tree. Once they attach themselves to a branch it is difficult to remove them.

It has an amazing flexible neck that can turn 180° in both the directions. This carnivore is most active at night and can see with amazing clarity at night.

318 Tiger

Tiger is the largest wild cat in the world. It is known the world over due to its orange-red coat with dark stripes. No two Tigers have the same pattern of stripes. It is found in forests and near swamps of India, China and Southeast Asia. It is about 6 feet in length with a long tail.

Tigers hunt alone and have excellent eyesight. Unlike other cats, Tigers are very good swimmers. When a Tiger walks, it does not leave its claw marks behind as it retracts its claws. It is a powerful predator and hunts alone.

319 Walrus

Walrus are found in the Arctic Sea. This large mammal which can grow from 7-11 feet in length spends most of its time in icy waters of the Arctic. It is also found sunbathing on the beach. This large mammal is seen in the hundreds lying on the beach.

Its coat is brown and wrinkled. It has two long tusks, bushy whiskers, flat flippers and bodies that are full of blubber. Its tusks can be as long as three feet! It uses its sensitive whiskers to sense its prey. Interestingly, it can lower down its heart beat to withstand the temperatures of the surrounding waters!

MAMMALS

320 Weasel

Weasels are native to North America, parts of South Africa, Europe, Asia and north of Africa. Weasels live in various habitats ranging from forests, meadows and even grasslands. Despite its size, a weasel is a powerful predator.

It has a long, slender body with short legs. It can move easily between small, confined places due to its flexible spine and short legs. Weasels can be 13-41 cms long with a long or a small tail. It has a brown or a black colour coat. It is a carnivore that preys on mice, squirrel, rabbit and hare, birds and insects. It lives in tree roots, crevices and burrows.

177

MAMMALS

321 Wolf

Wolf is the largest member of the dog family. It is found in North America, Europe and Asia. It is known the world over for its spine chilling howls. The howl is a way to communicate with other wolves and it is picked up by other wolves as a means to alert other groups or packs of wolves.

The Gray Wolf is the largest wolf of the species. It is the most common wolf. It can be 2-5 feet long with a long, bushy tail. It has sharp, canine teeth. It has a good eyesight, acute hearing and a keen sense of smell. It always hunts in packs and can travel up to 12 miles a day to search for its food.

322 Yak

Yak is found in Central Asia. Its habitat includes the mountains. Its body is covered in long hair which keep it warm. It is a herd animal. It has been domesticated for a long time. It is a herbivore with sharp horns. Both male and females have horns. It can climb 6,100 metre above sea level. It is also used to carry burden. It migrates seasonally to the lower plains for food and returns to the higher altitudes when it gets warmer in the lower plains.

323 Zebra

Zebras are native to the African grasslands. It is a herd animal and is found in large herds. It is a fast running mammal. It can grow up to 5 feet at the shoulder.

The most striking feature of the Zebra is its stripes. The black and white stripes are unique to each animal. Its stripes are used to camouflage itself and are also used to identify each other in a herd. It grazes grasses in large herds. Even in a herd, some Zebras keep a look for predators while the others graze.

324 Zorro

Zorro is native to the forests of South Africa. Due to its small ears, it is also called small-eared fox or a small-eared dog. It likes to stay near the forests, plains and shrub area. It is about 2-3 feet long with a long tail. It has a pointed muzzle and a bushy tail and its coat is brown in colour.

It comes out mostly at night. It eats rodents, birds, rabbits along with seeds and berries. It lives in burrows and abandoned dens.

MAMMALS

MARSUPIALS

325 Bandicoot

Bandicoot is a small creature that is native to Australia and New Guinea. Its habitat includes plains, forests, grasslands and even deserts.

It has a long, pointy nose. It measures between 11-32 inches at the shoulder and has a 3-7 inch long tail. It digs burrows with its sharp, clawed feet. It has a grey or brown coat. It is an omnivore which means that it eats both plants and smaller animals. It is a nocturnal animal. Like the kangaroos, its baby too grows up in the pouch of the female. Its pouch grows from the rear. It protects the young when the mother is digging.

326 Bilby

Bibly is native to the Australian continent. Bilby inhabits deserts, forests, dry shrubs and grasslands. It is a big eared marsupial that looks like a rabbit. It too is a burrowing animal.

It has strong, clawed feet. It is a solitary animal that digs extensive burrows. Its burrows can be up to 5 feet long. It has an excellent sense of smell and hearing though its eyesight is quite poor. It is an omnivore that eats small insects, mice, worms, fruits, nuts and plants. It gets most of its water from the food it eats. Thus, it drinks very less water.

MARSUPIALS

327 Kangaroo

Kangaroo, the largest marsupial, is native to Australia. It stands up to 6 feet tall. Instead of walking, it hops everywhere. It is also fondly called 'roos'.

Its front legs are small but its hind legs are long and powerful. It also has a long and strong tail. When standing, it uses its tail as another leg. It has large feet and can hop 30 feet in one bound. It can hop with a speed up to 40 mph. It lives in small groups called mobs. Female Kangaroos have a pouch in which it carries its baby called 'Joey'.

It is a herbivore and eats grass, leaves and roots. Did you know that it can go months without drinking water!

328 Koala

Koala is a small marsupial and native to Australia. It is often thought to be a kind of bear but it is actually related to the wombats. It stays on eucalyptus trees and either rests or sleeps for 18-20 hours.

Like Kangaroos, koala mothers too carry their newborn in their backward facing pouch for about six months. When the baby is grown enough, the mother carries the baby on her back until it is a year old.

When awake, it eats lots of eucalyptus leaves. It dines mostly at night. It is about 2-3 feet in length. Its fur is usually light brown to grey. It has rough pads on its hands and feet which help it to grab the branches of the tree.

MARSUPIALS

329 Nabarlek

Nabarlek is a small marsupial that is native to northern Australia. It is a kind of wallaby. Its habitat includes grasslands and small vegetation. It appears like a small kangaroo.

It has powerful and long hindlegs. Its forelegs are small. It has a strong tail which it uses to support itself when standing. The tail also balances it when it jumps. It can hop or jump. It can measure 20-25 inches in length. Its fur is light brown in colour. The females of the species have a pouch on their belly where it keeps the young for 26 weeks.

330 Numbat

Numbat is another small marsupial that is native to southern Australia. It inhabits woodlands and forests. It is among those marsupials that are most active during the day. At night, it stays in hollow logs to sleep and to seek shelter.

It feeds on termites and can eat as many as 2,000 termites in a day. It has a long tongue which it uses to reach the termites. Its front claws are also very strong. It can be between 13-18 inches in length. It has a long tail and has black and white stripes across its back. Though it is a marsupial but the females do not have a pouch to keep its young.

MARSUPIALS

331 Quokka

Quokka is also native to the Australian continent. It is among the smallest wallaby species in the world. It has a small tail that barely has fur on it and it has small hindlegs.

It has a small stocky body and looks hunched. Though it has short hindlegs, they are powerful which help it to hop. Unlike other marsupials, it can also climb trees. It can be 3 feet in length. It is a herbivore that eats leaves, seeds and roots. Due to its harsh habitat, it has adapted itself remarkably. It can thus go without water for months at a time.

332 Quoll

Quoll is native to Australia, Papua New Guinea and Tasmania. Its appearance is similar to that of a cat. It is found in woodlands, shrubs and grasses. It is a nocturnal animal.

It is about 2 feet in length. It has a long, hairy tail. It has white spots all over its body and also on its tail. It is a carnivore and the dominant predator in its habitat. It spends its day in a burrow or among rock piles. It feeds on insects but can also prey upon rabbits and mice.

MARSUPIALS

333 Ringtail Possum

Ringtail Possum is native to the temperate forests and rainforests of Australia, New Guinea and Tasmania. It is a tree dwelling marsupial which is most active at night. During the day, it sleeps in hollow trees or in nests made of leaves and twigs.

It has a long, prehensile tail that is one third white in colour. It uses its tail like a fifth limb when it climbs. It has an excellent sense of smell. It is between 16-46 cms in length with an equally long tail. Out of its five fingers, two are opposable. The young live in the female's pouch until matured. It is a herbivore. Did you know that it can even detoxify the toxicity of the eucalyptus leaves!

334 Sugar Glider

Sugar Gliders are native to Australia, Indonesia and New Guinea. Its habitat includes forests. It is called so because it likes to eat flowers and its nectar. It however also eats insects. It is most active during the night. Its scientific names means 'short headed rope dancer.'

It can glide to about 90 cms between trees. It has thin flaps of skin between its wrist and ankle which allow it to glide from tree to tree. It is about 20 cms in length with an equally long tail. It can use its long tail to steer itself in the air when gliding.

335 Tasmanian Devil

Tasmanian Devil is native to the Tasmania region of Australia. It inhabits forests and shrublands. It is called so because of its violent manner of defending its food and also because of the shrieking noises and snarls that it makes.

It is a solitary animal and is a carnivore. It comes out of its burrow at night to eat. It can be 51-79 cms in length. Its coat is of black or brown fur. It has powerful jaws that can even break bones. It is the largest carnivore marsupial. It can eat anything it can get. A young stays with the mother for 7-8 months until it becomes independent.

MARSUPIALS

336 Virginia Opossum

Virginia Opossum is native to North America. It inhabits the deciduous forests and prairies of eastern and western North America. This small marsupial is most active at night.

It is 2.5 feet in length with a long tail. It is famous for 'playing possum'. When threatened by a predator, it lies down on its side barely breathing, with its tongue sticking out and its eyes either stare into space or they are closed. This strategy helps it to confuse its predator and escape. It is an omnivore. It is very skillful in climbing trees. It is also a scavenger and is seen in people's homes.

MARSUPIALS

337 Wallaby

Wallabies are native to Australia and its nearby islands. It is a small to medium size marsupial. It can grow up to be 6 feet in length. It has powerful legs that allow it to hop. Its long tail supports it to sit or is often used as a fifth limb. The males also use its hindlegs to kick each other during a fight.

The young are born underdeveloped. It spends months in the mother's pouch as it grows. It is a herbivore which eats grasses, leaves and berries.

338 Wombat

Wombat, a native of Australia and its adjacent islands, inhabits the dry regions of the continent. It is a large and chubby marsupial. It is most active at night. It is about 2.5-3.5 feet in length. It has strong, sharp claws which it uses to dig its extensive burrows. It digs in grasslands and eucalyptus forests, causing quite a nuisance for farmers. It has incisors, resembling the rodents that continue to grow. It is a herbivore.

The females have a backward pouch where the underdeveloped young stay. It is a social animal and many wombats lives in one burrow.

339 American Alligator

The American Alligator is the biggest reptile in North America. Its skin is prized for leather goods, and the species was hunted nearly to extinction before laws were passed to protect them in the 1960s. Today, Alligators often can be seen basking in the sun near water in the south-eastern United States. A young Alligator can be distinguished by its distinct yellow stripes. Alligators dig deep holes in wetlands, which fill up with groundwater and help other wildlife survive droughts. These are called gator holes. It is however during the cold that the Alligators use these holes to stay inside them.

REPTILE

340 Black Caiman

Black Caimans are large, meat-eating reptiles that spend most of their lives in the water. They live in freshwater habitats in South America including the Amazon basin. They are very similar to the American Alligator. Caimans swim very well, using their webbed feet and long tail. Black Caimans are most active at night and hunt during that time. They have sensitive skin because they are adapted to live in the water where the sun doesn't burn. If exposure to sun is for too long, their skin becomes dry and starts shedding. Black Caiman's 75 long, sharp, conical teeth are used for catching their prey.

REPTILE

341 Black Mamba

The Black Mamba snake is one of Africa's most dangerous and feared snakes. The Black Mamba is the largest venomous snake in Africa and the second largest snake in the world, after the King Cobra. Adult Black Mambas have a maximum length of 4.5 m or around 14 feet. The Black Mamba is also the fastest land snake in the world. It can reach speeds in excess of 12 mph. It mainly uses this speed to escape danger rather than capturing its prey. The Black Mamba gets its name not because of the colour of its body, but because it has a blue-black colour mouth which it displays when it gets threatened.

342 Cantor's Giant Soft-shelled Turtle

This peculiar-looking species is a freshwater turtle that has a broad head and small eyes close to the tip of its snout. It can grow up to about 2 m in length and weigh more than 50 kg. The unusual turtle spends 95 per cent of its life buried and motionless, with only its eyes and mouth protruding from the sand. It comes on surface only twice a day to take a breath.

It lives in a variety of habitats and the species is found from peninsular India to China and Southeast Asia.

343 Chameleons

Chameleon is a type of lizard that has the ability to change the colour of its skin with the temperature, light and the chameleon's emotional level. They become paler when excited, afraid or in the dark or cold; they become darker when angry or in hot temperatures or in bright light.

Chameleons have a long, prehensile tail and a helmet-like casque on the head. They have a tremendously long, sticky tongue that is longer than their body! It is an insectivore and uses its long, sticky tongue to catch its prey. They are found almost everywhere in the world.

344 Chuckwalla

Chuckwalla lizard living in the southern United States has several unique features. These include a blanket of skin that covers its back. In the early morning, its skin is dark to attract sunlight which warms its blood. During the day, as the desert environment becomes extremely hot its skin changes to a beige colour and this prevents the lizard from getting overheated. A Chuckwalla will scurry away from predators to hide in tight cracks and will then puff its body out to fill the space making it nearly impossible to remove it.

REPTILE

345 Desert Tortoise

The Desert Tortoise is a timid reptile that lives in the sandy deserts of southwestern North America. It can live from 50 to 80 years. The Desert Tortoise spends most of its lifetime underground. It makes burrows to protect itself from extreme desert temperatures. As a herbivore, it eats grasses and all kinds of desert plants. Interestingly, adult Desert Tortoises can live without water for a year!

It has a hard upper shell about 9 to 15 inches long. It has a gular horn that extends from the front of the plastron (lower shell). When males fight other males, they use the gular horn to overturn an opponent.

346 Frilled Lizard

Frilled Lizards or 'frillnecks' are primarily found in North Australia and New Guinea. It has a large, thin frill around its head which it displays in order to frighten its enemies. To frighten its enemies more, it also opens its mouth wide and often rears up on its hind legs and hisses. When frightened, it runs away using only its back legs. Due to this habit, it is also called "bicycle lizard." These lizards live most of their lives on trees and are carnivores. When the lizard is at rest the frill folds down and rests on the lizard's shoulders.